THE
RANDOM HOUSE
BARBECUE
AND SUMMER FOODS
COOKBOOK

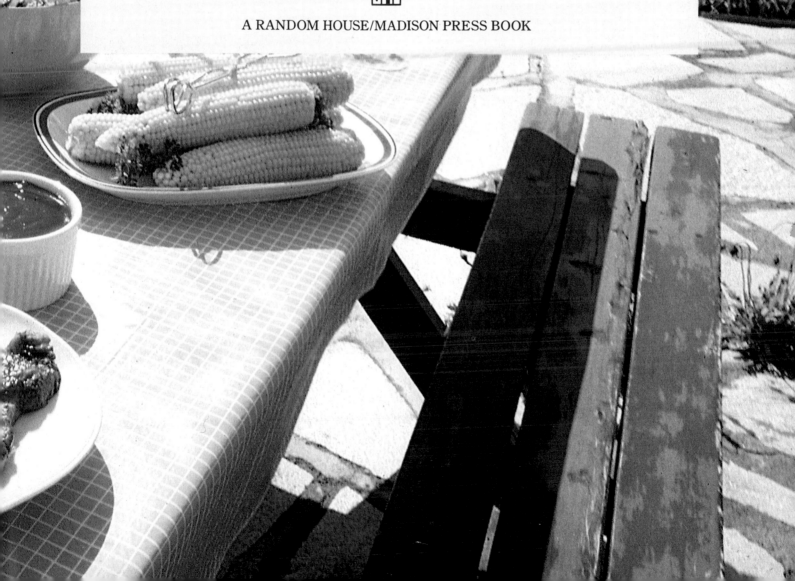

THE RANDOM HOUSE BARBECUE AND SUMMER FOODS COOKBOOK

By Margaret Fraser

A RANDOM HOUSE/MADISON PRESS BOOK

Library of Congress Cataloguing-in-Publication Data

Fraser, Margaret
  The Random house barbecue and summer foods cookbook

Originally published: The Canadian living barbecue and summer foods cookbook/by Margaret Fraser and the food writers of Canadian living magazine. 1988.

1. Barbecue cookery. 2. Outdoor cookery. I. Title.

TX840.B3F73 1989   641.5'784   90-8266
ISBN 0-394-58805-3

Manufactured in Italy
98765432
First American edition

On our cover: Barbecued chicken with Ginger Orange Sauce (p. 97) and Tangy Tomato Sauce (p. 96); Hoisin-Ginger Chicken Wings (p. 77).

**Produced by
Madison Press Books
40 Madison Avenue
Toronto, Ontario
Canada
M5R 2S1**

Contents

Introduction

Good times, good friends and great food are what you want when you barbecue. And that's what this book will help you achieve!

Americans love summertime, and lighting up the barbecue is a natural for meals that are spur-of-the-moment gatherings, planned neighborhood feasts, or upscale patio dinner parties. Coast to coast, we love to cook out-of-doors, anything from Pacific salmon to New England clams, from the South's ribs and briskets to good old steak, from kabobs to smoked pork loin, from turkey to Cornish hens. And best of all, we do burgers and hotdogs, fresh-caught fish from our rivers, lakes, and oceans, and chicken—any style.

With so many Americans barbecuing, our team of food writers and test kitchen staff have created recipes for every style of barbecuing, from grilling to smoking. We use all sizes of barbecues, from hibachis to fancy wagon models. We vary the fuels from charcoal to natural or propane gas. And of course, we often add hardwood chips and chunks or fresh herbs to the coals, for added flavor.

Summer cooking should be easy and foods that complement barbecued dishes include lots of make-ahead dishes. In this book, we offer recipes for tasty appetizers, zesty marinades and sauces, crisp salads and dressings, and refreshing desserts.

To make warm-weather dining even easier for you, you'll find ten complete menus that demonstrate how easy it is to prepare such perfect summer meals as a no-fuss Kids'-Style Barbecue, an elegant Poolside Dinner Party and even a fun Christmas Dinner in July with barbecued turkey as the centrepiece.

In the Barbecue Basics section, there's everything you always wanted to know about barbecuing. We offer advice on buying a barbecue, differences in fuels are explained, and there's up-to-date information about accessories. Throughout the book you'll find helpful hints for better barbecuing, reference tables to take the guesswork out of grilling and ideas for serving and presentation.

Whether novice or pro, beginner or year-round expert, if you grill, spit-roast, smoke-cook or just plain barbecue, *The Random House Barbecue and Summer Foods Cookbook* will add to your collection of favorite recipes. So light up the barbecue, relax in the great outdoors and savor the aroma and tastes of today's abundance of fresh foods. Enjoy!

Margaret Fraser

Barbecue Menus

Here are ten great barbecue menus to enjoy come rain or shine. Try the Western Barbecue (p.19) or Pot Luck Barbecue Dinner (p.12) when you're entertaining a crowd. And our Fourth of July Celebration Picnic (p.22) and Labor Day Supper (p.26) are perfect for those special long weekend parties. The Elegant Grilled Dinner (p.16) is a sophisticated menu for six to eight. We've even included an easy and fun burger-and-hotdog supper that the kids can help grill. Experiment with our recipes and your own combinations and celebrate the summer!

Create your own fabulous summer barbecue menu with great ingredients like succulent salmon, garden-fresh vegetables and French bread.

Lunch on the Patio

FOR EIGHT

Here's an easy menu for a relaxed lunch or brunch in the garden, on the patio, or even indoors. The cold soup, vegetable platter and dessert can be prepared in advance. Just before serving, arrange the vegetables on the platter, ladle the soup into pretty mugs or glasses and garnish the cheesecake. The chicken cooks on the barbecue as you and your guests sip the refreshing soup.

CHILLED CANTALOUPE SOUP
(recipe, p. 40)

CHILI CHICKEN*

VEGETABLE VINAIGRETTE PLATTER*

PIÑA COLADA CHEESECAKE
(recipe, p. 143)

*Recipes appear on opposite page.

Chili Chicken; Piña Colada Cheesecake; Vegetable Vinaigrette Platter

CHILI CHICKEN

The barbecue sauce in this dish is medium-hot (increase the pepper flakes or add hot pepper sauce if you want it hotter). You can use Cornish hens, chicken quarters or turkey parts.

2 cups	thick chili sauce	500 mL
1 cup	chicken stock	250 mL
1/2 cup	cider vinegar	125 mL
4	cloves garlic, minced	4
1 tbsp	Worcestershire sauce	15 mL
1 tbsp	chili powder	15 mL
2 tsp	paprika	10 mL
2 tsp	hot pepper flakes	10 mL
1 tsp	salt	5 mL
1 tsp	ground cumin	5 mL
1/2 tsp	ground allspice	2 mL
1/2 tsp	cayenne pepper	2 mL
1/2 tsp	black pepper	2 mL
4	Cornish hens, split*	4

• In saucepan, combine chili sauce, chicken stock, vinegar, garlic, Worcestershire sauce, chili powder, paprika, hot pepper flakes, salt, cumin, allspice, cayenne and black pepper; simmer for 10 minutes and let cool.

• Place chicken in shallow pan; pour sauce over. Cover and marinate in refrigerator for 4 to 8 hours, turning once or twice.

• Transfer chicken to shallow baking pan; spoon about half the sauce on top. Bake in 350°F (180°C) oven for 45 minutes or until nearly tender. (Alternatively, microwave chicken, 4 halves at a time, at Medium/50% for about 40 minutes.)

• Then cook over hot coals or on high setting, turning once or twice and brushing often with remaining sauce, for about 10 minutes or until skin is crisp and well-browned. Makes 8 servings.

*To split hens: With poultry shears or large knife, remove backbone by cutting along one side from tail to neck, then along other side. Place bird breast side up; with your hand or flat side of cleaver, press firmly to break breastbone and flatten bird. Cut in half lengthwise.

VEGETABLE VINAIGRETTE PLATTER

This colorful vegetable dish is easy to prepare. Use whatever fresh vegetables are available, including at least three kinds, with contrasting colors and shapes.

2 lb	fresh asparagus	1 kg
1 lb	tiny green beans	500 g
1 lb	baby carrots	500 g
1 lb	tiny white mushrooms	500 g
	Lettuce leaves	
1	large red onion	1
	Chopped fresh parsley	
VINAIGRETTE:		
1 cup	vegetable oil	250 mL
1/4 cup	white or white wine vinegar	50 mL
1/4 cup	lemon juice	50 mL
2	cloves garlic, minced	2
1	small onion, minced	1
1/2 tsp	salt	2 mL
	Pepper	

• Trim vegetables. In saucepan of boiling salted water, cook asparagus, beans and carrots separately just until tender-crisp. Drain and chill quickly in cold water; drain again thoroughly. Place vegetables and mushrooms in separate shallow bowls.

• **Vinaigrette:** Whisk together oil, vinegar, lemon juice, garlic, onion, salt, and pepper to taste. Pour over vegetables and mushrooms; marinate in refrigerator for at least 2 hours, turning vegetables once or twice. Drain and reserve dressing.

• Arrange vegetables on lettuce-lined large platter (alternatively, salad greens can be served in separate bowl). Slice red onion thinly and separate into rings; scatter over vegetables. Sprinkle lightly with chopped parsley. Drizzle enough dressing over vegetables to moisten; serve remaining dressing separately. Makes about 8 servings.

Kids'-Style Barbecue

FOR SIX TO EIGHT

School's out and the kids are everywhere. They're in the backyard, on the deck, at the park—and especially, around with their friends at mealtimes. Here's a menu that lets the kids help with the cooking. Start them off with crunchy vegetable sticks and a dip you can serve in a cabbage for fun. Then move them on to the feature attraction—burgers and hotdogs in imaginative presentations. Finish with a frosty dessert.

FRESH VEGETABLES AND WATERCRESS CUCUMBER DIP
(sidebar, p. 33)

MEXICALI BURGERS*

SAUSAGE BAVARIAN STYLE
(recipe, p. 71)

BURGERBOBS*

ASSORTED BUNS AND BREADS

BANANA-YOGURT BOATS
(recipe, p. 146)
or

ICE CREAM SANDWICHES
(recipe, p. 146)

*Recipes appear on these two pages.

Burgerbobs, hotdogs and sausages on the grill; fresh vegetables; Watercress Cucumber Dip in a cabbage

---

MEXICALI BURGERS

A taste of Mexico, but burger style instead of taco style.

1 lb	ground beef	500 g
1 tsp	salt	5 mL
	Pepper	
4	hamburger buns	4
TOPPINGS:		
4	slices bacon	4
1	small avocado	1
	Lemon juice	
1	small tomato, peeled and chopped	1
1	jalapeño pepper, chopped (optional)	1
2 tbsp	chopped onion	25 mL
1/2 tsp	salt	2 mL

• Mix beef with 1 tsp (5 mL) salt, and pepper to taste; shape into 4 patties.

• **Toppings:** Cook bacon and drain well; crumble and set aside in small bowl. Peel and slice avocado thinly; brush with lemon juice and set aside in another bowl. In third bowl, combine tomato, jalapeño pepper (if using), onion and salt.

• Cook patties on greased grill over hot coals or on high setting to desired doneness. Toast buns lightly. Place patties in buns and serve with choice of toppings. Makes 4 servings.

Dips are a great way to get kids to eat their vegetables. Serve them in hollowed-out cabbages with an assortment of crunchy carrot sticks, broccoli and cauliflower florets, celery, green beans, cherry tomatoes and breadsticks or crackers. To hollow out a cabbage, choose a small Savoy, red or green cabbage and discard any discolored outer leaves. With a sharp knife, cut out the core of the cabbage, then scoop out enough of the interior to hold the dip. Use what you scooped out to make coleslaw. You may have to cut a slice from the bottom of the cabbage so that it sits flat on your serving plate.

BURGERBOBS

Warm pita breads in foil on the edge of the barbecue. Slip burgerbobs from skewers into pita pockets and top with chopped cucumber.

1-1/2 lb	lean ground beef	750 g
1	small onion, finely chopped	1
1	egg, beaten	1
1 tbsp	fresh coriander	15 mL
1/2 tsp	ground cumin	2 mL
	Salt and pepper	
1 cup	ketchup	250 mL
1 tbsp	prepared horseradish	15 mL
1/2 tsp	Worcestershire sauce	2 mL
4	pita bread	4
1/2 cup	chopped cucumber	125 mL

• In large bowl, combine beef, onion, egg, coriander, cumin, and salt and pepper to taste. Mix well and shape into 16 meatballs. Thread onto greased metal skewers.

• In small bowl, blend ketchup, horseradish and Worcestershire sauce.

• Cook meatballs on greased grill over hot coals or on high setting, brushing generously with ketchup sauce, to desired doneness. Remove from skewers and place 4 meatballs in each pita; top with cucumber. Makes 4 servings.

Pot Luck Barbecue Dinner

FOR TWENTY

Pot luck dinners are here to stay. With today's hectic schedules, it's the perfect way to enjoy the pleasure of being with special friends. Each guest brings a dish and joins in the fun. The Fruit-Filled Watermelon is a great crowd-pleasing dessert—and so are the luscious cakes.

TARAMA DEVILLED EGGS *(recipe, p. 30)*	**FRUIT-FILLED WATERMELON WITH** **LEMON-LIME SYRUP** *(recipe, p. 133)*
TECHNICOLOR VEGETABLE **ANTIPASTO** *(recipe, p. 33)*	*or*
SUMMER SANGRIA *(recipe, p. 42)*	**KIWI TORTE, ORANGE CHIFFON ROLL** **WITH MANGO-LIME CURD, AND** **TROPICAL CHEESECAKE WITH** **GINGER-COCONUT CRUST** *(recipes, pp. 137,140,139)*
ALMOND SOUP WITH ORANGE ZEST *(recipe, p. 39)*	
HERBED LEMON SPARERIBS*	
NEW POTATO SALAD WITH CELERY *(recipe, p. 121)*	**Recipes appear on opposite page.*
GRATED ZUCCHINI SAUTÉ*	

HERBED LEMON SPARERIBS

Look for the meatiest ribs when planning a barbecue. Back ribs are best but side ribs, if not trimmed too close to the bone, make a succulent feast.

10 lb	pork spareribs	4.5 kg
2 cups	vegetable oil (preferably olive)	500 mL
18	cloves garlic, minced	18
1 cup	finely chopped fresh parsley	250 mL
1/3 cup	coarsely grated lemon rind	75 mL
1 cup	lemon juice	250 mL
3 tbsp	crumbled dried thyme	50 mL
2 tbsp	each crumbled dried rosemary, sage, savory and marjoram	25 mL
2 tsp	black pepper	10 mL
1 tsp	crumbled dried mint	5 mL
1 tsp	each ground allspice and cumin	5 mL
1/2 tsp	cayenne pepper	2 mL
	Salt	
GARNISH:		
4	lemons	4
	Strips of lemon rind and thyme sprigs (optional)	

- In large stockpot, cover ribs with boiling water; cover and bring to boil. Reduce heat and simmer for 45 to 60 minutes or until ribs are tender. Drain and let cool; pack into large heavy plastic bag.
- Combine oil, garlic, parsley, lemon rind, lemon juice, thyme, rosemary, sage, savory, marjoram, pepper, mint, allspice, cumin and cayenne; pour over ribs, coating meat evenly. Tie bag closed, place in large bowl and marinate in refrigerator for 8 to 24 hours, turning bag over periodically. (Note: There is just enough marinade to cover ribs, not to swish around.)
- Remove ribs, reserving any marinade; bring ribs to room temperature. Cook on greased grill over hot coals or on high setting for about 10 minutes per side or until meat comes away from bone, brushing occasionally with any marinade. Season with salt to taste after cooking. Cut into serving-sized portions of 3 to 4 ribs.
- **Garnish:** Cut lemons into wedges. Garnish ribs with lemon wedges, and lemon rind and thyme (if using). Makes 20 servings.

GRATED ZUCCHINI SAUTÉ

This hot vegetable dish is a pleasant change from just another buffet salad.

4-3/4 lb	zucchini (about 16)	2.15 kg
1 cup	butter	250 mL
8	large cloves garlic, minced	8
1 tbsp	chopped fresh tarragon (or 1 tsp/ 5 mL dried)	15 mL
2 tsp	Dijon mustard	10 mL
1/2 tsp	salt	2 mL
GARNISH (optional):		
	Tarragon sprigs Tomato rose	

- Trim and grate zucchini coarsely.
- In two very large skillets, melt butter over low heat; cook garlic for 5 minutes or until softened, stirring frequently. Add tarragon, mustard and salt. Increase heat to medium and stir in zucchini; cook, stirring frequently, for 15 to 20 minutes or until most of the liquid has evaporated. Reduce heat to low and cook, stirring frequently, until all liquid has evaporated, about 10 minutes. Taste and adjust seasoning if necessary. (Recipe can be prepared to this point, cooled, covered and refrigerated for up to 8 hours. Reheat over medium-low heat, stirring frequently.)
- **Garnish:** Transfer to serving bowl; garnish with tarragon and tomato rose if desired. Makes 20 servings.

Christmas Dinner in July

FOR SIX

Our festive menu begins with elegant smoked salmon appetizers. The traditional turkey can be presented hot from the barbecue or sliced and served cold. There's mincemeat, too—served over ice cream for a refreshing change. The ideal beverage? Pitchers filled with Cranberry Iced Tea. Whether you want to recapture the delicious flavors and warmth of a holiday dinner with family or friends, or just enjoy good food, you'll love these ideas.

CRANBERRY ICED TEA
(recipe, p. 45)

SMOKED SALMON WRAP-UPS*

SPIT-ROASTED TURKEY*

MIXED GREENS WITH SEASONED CROUTONS
(sidebar this page)

RATATOUILLE
(recipe, p. 122)

ICE CREAM WITH HOT MINCEMEAT SAUCE

*Recipes appear on these two pages.

Cranberry Iced Tea; Spit-Roasted Turkey

SMOKED SALMON WRAP-UPS

Hearts of palm are available, canned, in the specialty section of large supermarkets. If you can't get them, you can substitute asparagus. (photo, p.29)

3 cups	packed fresh spinach	750 mL
2 tbsp	mayonnaise	25 mL
2 tbsp	plain yogurt	25 mL
1 tsp	Dijon mustard	5 mL
	Salt and pepper	
1/2 lb	smoked salmon, sliced	250 g
1	can (410 g) hearts of palm, drained	1
	Black olives, dill sprigs, lemon rind (optional)	

• Trim stems and coarse leaves from spinach; rinse well. In large saucepan, cook spinach with just the water clinging to leaves for 3 to 5 minutes or just until wilted. Rinse under cold water; drain well and squeeze spinach dry. Chop finely.
• In bowl, mix together spinach, mayonnaise, yogurt, mustard, and salt and pepper to taste.
• Lay enough salmon slices together to make 6- x 3-1/2-inch (15 x 9 cm) rectangle, tucking in loose ends and overlapping slices slightly. Spread about 2 tbsp (25 mL) spinach mixture evenly over rectangle. Place 1 or 2 hearts of palm (depending on thickness) at narrow end of salmon. Roll up tightly, tucking in sides if necessary. Repeat with remaining salmon. You should have about 5 rolls. Cover rolls with plastic wrap; refrigerate for at least 1 hour or up to 8 hours.
• At serving time, cut rolls diagonally into 1/2-inch (1 cm) thick slices. Garnish with olives, dill and lemon rind (if using). Makes about 30 hors d'oeuvres.

SEASONED CROUTONS

For a hint of turkey dressing flavor, make these seasoned croutons for your salad. Cut 4 slices French bread into 1/2-inch (1 cm) cubes. In large skillet, melt 1/4 cup (50 mL) butter over medium heat. Add 1 garlic clove and toss in butter for 1 minute. Add

bread cubes and cook, stirring occasionally, until bread is coated with butter and evenly toasted. Sprinkle 1/4 tsp (1 mL) each dried thyme, dried sage and salt, and pepper to taste over cubes, tossing to distribute evenly. Remove garlic clove. Set cubes aside to cool. Makes 2 cups (500 mL).

SPIT-ROASTED TURKEY

If roast turkey is a must for your festive dinner, even in July, make the dinner easy, summery and casual. Get out of the kitchen and barbecue the turkey.

• To spit-roast the turkey, grease the bird inside and out, and truss (tie) it into a tight shape that balances easily on the spit. It's better to put two small turkeys on a spit rather than one that's too large. The cavity can be filled with onion, lemon or orange slices, sprigs of fresh herbs or sprinklings of dried herbs; regular stuffings don't cook properly with this method.

• Be sure to have a drip pan under the bird and use the drippings to baste it. As a guideline, a 3- to 4-lb (1.5 to 2 kg) bird will take about 1-1/2 hours to spit-roast; a 6- to 8-lb (3 to 4 kg) bird will take 2-1/2 to 3 hours over medium-hot coals or on medium setting.

• For a covered barbecue (gas or charcoal), cook the bird stuffed or unstuffed. Place the bird on the grill over a drip pan nestled between two beds of hot coals. Roast until meat thermometer inserted in thickest part of inner thigh registers 185°F (85°C).

Elegant Grilled Dinner

FOR SIX TO EIGHT

Whether served indoors on elegant damask or outdoors on the patio table, this sophisticated dinner menu is great in any setting. Much of it can be prepared in advance. Three of the dishes are quickly grilled just before serving. The simple Honey-Yogurt Sauce poured over sliced seasonal fruit provides a light and lovely finish.

LEMON GRILLED SHRIMP
(recipe, p. 35)

BAKED GOAT CHEESE WITH WATERCRESS SAUCE
(recipe, p. 35)

GRILLED LAMB LOINS WITH ROASTED PEPPER AND GARLIC SAUCE*

GRILLED ONION SALAD
(recipe, p. 121)

GREEN BEANS WITH TOASTED PINE NUTS
(recipe, p. 124)

CRISP POTATO ROSES
(recipe, p. 119)

FRUIT WITH HONEY-YOGURT SAUCE
(recipe, p. 140)

*Recipe appears on these two pages.

GRILLED LAMB LOINS WITH ROASTED PEPPER AND GARLIC SAUCE

The delicate flavor of lamb could easily be overpowered by overly assertive flavoring agents, so try just a hint of mesquite, rosemary, spices or grapevine clippings sprinkled on the hot coals.

3 lb	boneless lamb loins	1.5 kg
1/4 cup	olive oil	50 mL
2 tbsp	lemon juice	25 mL
1	clove garlic, minced	1
	Pepper	
	Roasted Pepper and Garlic Sauce (recipe follows)	

• Place lamb in sturdy plastic bag set in bowl. Stir together oil, lemon juice, garlic, and pepper to taste; pour over lamb. Close bag tightly; squeeze gently to coat lamb well. Refrigerate for at least 6 hours or overnight, turning bag occasionally. Remove from refrigerator 30 to 45 minutes before grilling.

• Cook lamb on greased grill over medium-hot coals or on medium setting, basting often with marinade and turning once when red juices pool on top, for 3 to 5 minutes per side or until meat feels springy when pressed lightly with fingers protected with paper towels and is still pink in centre. Cover with foil and let stand for 10 to 15 minutes before slicing thinly on the diagonal.

• Meanwhile, reheat Roasted Pepper and Garlic Sauce over low heat, stirring often. Arrange slices of lamb on warm serving plates; spoon a little sauce onto each plate. Pass remaining sauce separately. Makes 8 servings.

(On dinner plate) Grilled Lamb Loins with Roasted Pepper and Garlic Sauce; Crisp Potato Roses; Green Beans with Toasted Pine Nuts; (On salad plate) Grilled Onion Salad

ROASTED PEPPER AND GARLIC SAUCE:

1	head garlic	1
2 tsp	olive oil	10 mL
3	small sweet red peppers	3
Half	small hot red chili pepper	Half
1	small onion, halved	1
1/2 cup	whipping cream	125 mL
1/2 tsp	granulated sugar	2 mL
1/4 tsp	salt	1 mL

• Remove any papery layers from garlic head. Place garlic on piece of foil, drizzle with oil and wrap loosely. Cook on greased grill over coolest spot of medium-hot coals or on medium setting for 10 minutes. Add red and chili peppers and onion to centre of rack; cook, turning occasionally, for 20 to 30 minutes or until lightly charred, removing garlic when softened.

• Place peppers in paper bag; seal and let stand for 10 minutes. Remove charred outer layers from onion. Peel and seed peppers. In food processor or blender, combine peppers with onion. Squeeze soft pulp out of garlic head into food processor bowl; process until smooth. Add cream, sugar and salt; process until well blended. Transfer to small stainless steel saucepan; cover and refrigerate for up to 2 days. Makes about 1-1/2 cups (375 mL).

MARINATED CUCUMBER SALAD WITH RED ONIONS AND SOUR CREAM

This creamy make-ahead salad actually improves in flavor after it marinates for several hours.

2	seedless English cucumbers, sliced*	2
	Salt	
1	red onion, sliced	1
1/2 cup	sour cream	125 mL
2 tbsp	packed brown sugar	25 mL
2 tbsp	vinegar	25 mL
1/4 tsp	dry mustard	1 mL
	Dill (optional)	

• In glass bowl, layer cucumbers, sprinkling each layer with salt. Cover with plate that fits inside bowl. Weigh down and let stand for at least 3 hours at room temperature. Drain and rinse well. Drain again and pat dry. Separate onion slices into rings and stir into cucumbers.
• In small bowl, combine sour cream, sugar, vinegar and mustard. Pour over cucumber mixture and toss well. Cover and refrigerate until serving time, at least 2 hours. Garnish with dill (if using). Makes 8 to 10 servings.
*Peel cucumbers only if skin is bitter.

Western Barbecue
FOR EIGHT TO TEN

Wherever you live, celebrate summer the way they do down on the ranch, with a down-home party menu to be enjoyed outdoors. All of the dishes, except the centrepiece Spit-Roasted Prime Rib of Beef, are make-ahead easy. And don't forget to have plenty of cold beer and cider on hand!

CHERRY TOMATOES STUFFED WITH GUACAMOLE
(recipe, p. 36)

SPIT-ROASTED PRIME RIB OF BEEF WITH AIOLI SAUCE
(recipe, p. 51)

CORN MUFFINS WITH SWEET RED PEPPERS*

POTATO SALAD

MARINATED CUCUMBER SALAD
WITH RED ONIONS AND SOUR CREAM*

CHILLED GREEN PEA SALAD WITH DILL
(recipe, p. 117)

BLUEBERRY AND STRAWBERRY TART
(recipe, p. 128)

*Recipes appear on these two pages.

(Clockwise from top) Corn Muffins with Sweet Red Peppers; Chilled Green Pea Salad with Dill; Marinated Cucumber Salad with Red Onions and Sour Cream; Spit-Roasted Prime Rib of Beef with Aioli Sauce; Cherry Tomatoes Stuffed with Guacamole

CORN MUFFINS WITH SWEET RED PEPPERS

No western barbecue would be complete without corn bread. This variation includes red pepper, a natural accompaniment to corn bread.

1/2 cup	all-purpose flour	125 mL
1/2 cup	yellow cornmeal	125 mL
2 tbsp	granulated sugar	25 mL
2 tsp	baking powder	10 mL
1/2 tsp	salt	2 mL
1/2 tsp	pepper	2 mL
1/2 cup	buttermilk	125 mL
2 tbsp	vegetable oil	25 mL
1	egg	1
1/4 cup	finely chopped sweet red pepper	50 mL

• In large bowl, combine flour, cornmeal, sugar, baking powder, salt and pepper. In small bowl, beat together buttermilk, oil and egg; stir into dry ingredients just until moistened. Stir in red pepper.

• Spoon batter into well-greased or paper-lined muffin cups, filling each two-thirds full. Bake in 425°F (220°C) oven for 15 minutes or until tester inserted in centre comes out clean. (Alternatively, bake in 8-inch square/2 L baking pan in 425°F/220°C oven for 20 minutes or until firm to the touch. Cut into squares to serve.) Makes 12 muffins.

Poolside Dinner Party

FOR SIX

The beautiful presentation of grilled fish and shellfish is sure to make this menu part of your permanent summer repertoire. Everyone can have a taste of each—succulent shrimp, lobster, salmon and pike. Red potatoes on skewers can be barbecued alongside. A simple spinach and tomato salad and cheesy breadsticks are the perfect accompaniments.

CHEESY BREADSTICKS

SPINACH AND TOMATO SALAD

GRILLED SHELLFISH
(sidebar, p. 87)

GRILLED PIKE STRIPS WITH ORIENTAL MARINADE*

GRILLED SALMON STEAKS*

SKEWERED POTATOES
(sidebar opposite page)

LAYERED RASPBERRY PARFAITS
(recipe, p. 134)

*Recipes appear on these two pages.

GRILLED SALMON STEAKS

The best fish for the barbecue are those with distinctive flavors such as salmon, trout, mackerel and swordfish.

6	salmon steaks, 1 inch (2.5 cm) thick (about 2 lb/1 kg total)	6

MARINADE:

1/2 cup	vegetable oil	125 mL
1/4 cup	lemon juice	50 mL
1/4 cup	white vermouth	50 mL
2 tbsp	chopped onion	25 mL
1 tbsp	packed brown sugar	15 mL
1 tsp	dried tarragon or dillweed	5 mL
1/2 tsp	dry mustard	2 mL
1/2 tsp	salt	2 mL
	Pepper	

• Place fish in shallow dish.

• **Marinade:** In small bowl, mix together oil, lemon juice, vermouth, onion, sugar, tarragon, mustard, salt, and pepper to taste; pour over fish. Cover and let stand at room temperature for 2 hours, turning occasionally.

• Drain fish, reserving marinade. Cook on greased grill over hot coals or on high setting, turning once and basting often with marinade, for about 5 minutes on each side or until fish flakes easily when tested with fork. Makes 6 servings.

(On table) Grilled Shellfish; Grilled Pike Strips; Cheesy Breadsticks; Spinach and Tomato Salad; (On barbecue) Grilled Salmon Steaks; Skewered Potatoes

GRILLED PIKE STRIPS WITH ORIENTAL MARINADE

SKEWERED POTATOES

Lightly oil parboiled new potatoes. Thread onto long greased metal skewers. Grill over hot coals or on high setting for 3 minutes, turning often.

Use this marinade to baste fish on the barbecue as you turn the skewers over. Delicious on pork ribs, chicken pieces or beef kabobs, this same marinade complements many flavors.

1-1/2 lb	boneless pike fillets	750 g
MARINADE:		
1/4 cup	hoisin sauce*	50 mL
2 tbsp	granulated sugar	25 mL
2 tbsp	rice wine* or dry sherry	25 mL
1 tbsp	oyster sauce*	15 mL
1/2 tsp	salt	2 mL
1/2 tsp	five-spice powder*	2 mL

• **Marinade:** In small bowl, stir together hoisin sauce, sugar, rice wine, oyster sauce, salt and five-spice powder until sugar and salt are dissolved.

• Cut fish fillets in long strips, about 1 inch (2.5 cm) wide. Place in non-metallic dish; cover with marinade. Refrigerate for about 2 hours, turning several times.

• Thread marinated fish strips onto oiled skewers. Cook over hot coals or on high setting until fish is white and flakes easily, about 3 minutes on each side. Makes 6 servings.

*Available in oriental grocery stores.

Fourth of July Celebration Picnic

FOR EIGHT

What better way to celebrate the Fourth than with a barbecue picnic highlighting this country's splendid fruits and vegetables, beef and seafood! The Fireworks Barbecue Sauce is delicious on steak and its fire can be adjusted to your taste. Strawberries are the star of the summer season, so finish this picnic with a pretty Strawberry Tart.

SEAFOOD SALAD PLATTER AND VEGETABLE CRUDITÉS WITH HERBED MAYONNAISE*

SPARKLING LEMONADE
(recipe, p. 43)

GRILLED STEAK WITH FIREWORKS BARBECUE SAUCE
(recipe, p. 99)

SESAME ROLLS

NEW POTATOES IN GARLIC-BASIL BUTTER
(sidebar, p. 124)

SUPER SLAW
(recipe, p. 110)

STRAWBERRY TART
(recipe, p. 126)

Recipes appear on these two pages.

QUICK MAYONNAISE

This lovely, smooth mild mayonnaise is nearly foolproof and takes less than a minute in all. The only thing you can do wrong is add the oil too quickly at first, which means the mixture won't emulsify and thicken. If that happens, just pour mixture into a measuring cup, put another egg in the food processor, and with machine running, very gradually add the first mixture again. If you want to make a smaller amount, the recipe can be halved. Be sure to use very fresh oil.

2	eggs	2
3 tbsp	lemon juice or white wine vinegar	50 mL
3/4 tsp	salt	4 mL
3/4 tsp	dry mustard	4 mL
2-1/4 cups	vegetable oil	550 mL

• In food processor or blender, combine eggs, lemon juice, salt and mustard. Add 1/4 cup (50 mL) of the oil and process for about 5 seconds or until blended.
• With machine running, gradually add remaining oil in very thin stream, very slowly at first, then more quickly as mayonnaise starts to thicken. Store in covered jar in refrigerator. Makes about 2-1/2 cups (625 mL).

VARIATION:

HERBED MAYONNAISE:
• To 1 cup (250 mL) mayonnaise, add 2 tsp (10 mL) each finely minced fresh parsley, chives and fresh dill. Add a little salt or lemon juice to taste, if desired.

GRILLED STEAK

Prime cuts grilled to perfection can still be kept within your budget. Instead of buying one steak per person, buy one large thick (1-1/2 to 2 in/4 to 5 cm) tender steak, such as sirloin. A thick piece weighing about 2 lb (1 kg) can serve 4 or more people, and is tastier and juicier than thin steaks. Grill to rare or medium, brushing with Fireworks Barbecue Sauce (recipe, p. 99). Slice the steak across the grain into thin slices and serve topped with more sauce on hearty sesame buns.

VEGETABLE CRUDITÉS

For raw vegetable dippers, choose the skinniest asparagus, young green beans, tiny new carrots (or carrot sticks), celery stalks and green onions. Serve in an attractive cup or arrange on crushed ice. Serve with Herbed Mayonnaise for dipping.

If vegetables are to be added to the Seafood Salad Platter, they should be very lightly cooked (in boiling water), then chilled in ice water, and marinated in a little Vinaigrette Dressing.

(Clockwise from top)
Sparkling Lemonade; New
Potatoes in Garlic-Basil
Butter; Grilled Steak with
Fireworks Barbecue
Sauce; Seafood Salad
Platter and Vegetable
Crudités with Herbed
Mayonnaise; Super Slaw

SEAFOOD SALAD PLATTER

*Canada's sensational fish and seafood are
cause to celebrate all on their own. For a giant
appetizer platter, choose any combination of fish
and shellfish. Allow 1/4 to 1/2 pound (125 to
250 g) per person.*

• Marinate chunks or slices of cooked lobster
or crab, peeled and deveined cooked shrimp
and cooked scallops (cut in half, if large). Add
1-inch (2.5 cm) pieces of any cooked, firm-
fleshed fish such as salmon, halibut, cod or
whitefish. Be sure to remove skin and bones
from fish, if present.

• **Marinade/Vinaigrette Dressing:** After
cooking fish and shellfish, place each type in
separate bowl and toss lightly with marinade;
use about 1/4 cup (50 mL) per pound (500 g)
of fish. Cover and marinate in refrigerator for
at least 2 hours or up to 2 days. For 1 cup
(250 mL) marinade/dressing, combine 3/4 cup
(175 mL) vegetable oil, 1/4 cup (50 mL) lemon
juice, 1/4 cup (50 mL) chopped fresh parsley,
1 tbsp (15 mL) each chopped fresh dill and
chives, 1/2 tsp (2 mL) salt and pinch of
pepper.

• **To Serve:** Arrange fish and shellfish
attractively on lettuce-lined platter. Garnish as
desired with fresh dill, lemon or cucumber
slices. Vegetable Crudités may be arranged on
the same platter or served separately. Serve
with Herbed Mayonnaise.

Sunday Country House Dinner

FOR SIX TO EIGHT

Barbecuing and country houses go hand in hand. Here's an easy dinner menu composed of your favorite seasonal foods cooked simply. Grilled steak is enhanced with a Garlic and Black Olive Sauce. The vegetables can be cooked right on the barbecue or in the oven. And fruit for dessert—whether it's fresh strawberries and sweet cream or a light fruit salad—provides the perfect end to this satisfying dinner.

ASSORTED CHEESES AND CRACKERS

GRILLED STEAK WITH GARLIC AND BLACK OLIVE SAUCE*

ROASTED SUMMER VEGETABLES*

FRESH STRAWBERRIES AND CREAM
or
SUMMER FRUIT SALAD*

*Recipes appear on opposite page.

GRILLED STEAK WITH GARLIC AND BLACK OLIVE SAUCE

Everyone loves barbecued steak in the summer. The garlicky sauce enhances the meat's flavor.

2 lb	steak (rib, sirloin or T-bone)	1 kg
	Pepper	
	Italian parsley (optional)	
GARLIC AND BLACK OLIVE SAUCE:		
1 cup	butter	250 mL
10	cloves garlic, minced	10
1-1/2 cups	coarsely chopped black olives	375 mL

• **Garlic and Black Olive Sauce:** In saucepan, melt butter over low heat; add garlic and olives and cook until bubbly. Set saucepan on back of grill to keep warm.
• Sprinkle steak with pepper to taste; cook on greased grill over hot coals or on high setting until desired doneness, basting occasionally with sauce. Arrange on serving plates; pour sauce over or pour into sauceboat and pass separately. Garnish with parsley (if using). Makes 6 to 8 servings.

ROASTED SUMMER VEGETABLES

When the sun is shining, the last place you want to be is in the kitchen cooking vegetables. Here's an easy way to cook them right on the barbecue, provided the vegetables are large enough not to fall through the grill. They'll look shrivelled when they're done but taste delicious!

6 to 8	zucchini (each about 6 in/15 cm long)	6 to 8
8 to 10	baby carrots (each about 3 in/8 cm long)	8 to 10
8 to 10	small new potatoes	8 to 10
1/2 cup	olive oil	125 mL
2 tbsp	coarse salt	25 mL
	Italian parsley (optional)	

• Wash zucchini, carrots and potatoes, leaving stems and skins intact; dry well. Arrange on greased grill or place in shallow foil baking dish. (Alternatively, arrange in shallow baking dish.)
• Brush with oil and sprinkle with salt. Cook over medium-hot coals or on medium setting or bake in 375°F (190°C) oven for about 30 minutes or until vegetables are slightly browned and shrivelled. Garnish with parsley (if using). Makes 6 to 8 servings.

SUMMER FRUIT SALAD

This summery salad can be made well in advance. For a spirited version, add 2 tbsp (25 mL) kirsch to the yogurt mixture.

2 cups	pitted black cherries	500 mL
1 cup	gooseberries	250 mL
1 cup	blueberries	250 mL
3/4 cup	packed brown sugar	175 mL
	Juice of 2 limes	
1-1/2 cups	plain yogurt	375 mL
	Fresh mint leaves	

• In large bowl, combine cherries, gooseberries and blueberries; sprinkle with sugar and lime juice. Let stand for at least 2 hours, tossing occasionally.
• With slotted spoon, transfer fruit to small serving dishes or wine glasses. Stir yogurt into remaining juices in bowl; mix well. Spoon yogurt mixture over each serving. Garnish with mint. Makes 6 to 8 servings.

(Left to right) Assorted cheeses and crackers; fresh strawberries and cream; Grilled Steak with Garlic and Black Olive Sauce; Roasted Summer Vegetables

MEAL PLANNING AT THE COUNTRY HOUSE

Plan to use the barbecue for several dinners during the week; barbecuing is a talent that teens can easily master and it keeps the kitchen tidy and cool. Make a schedule of duties the first day so everyone helps with meal preparation and cleanup.

Labor Day Supper
FOR FOUR

Start this perfect end-of-summer supper with a cool, delicious gazpacho. The pork chops and vegetables are marinated together in an oriental-flavored marinade that can be thickened into a sauce to accompany the dish. It's a casual meal to be enjoyed at sunset out-of-doors or inside.

SUMMER GAZPACHO
(recipe, p. 39)

GINGERED PORK CHOPS AND SKEWERED VEGETABLES*

SPINACH SALAD

GARLIC TOASTS
(sidebar opposite page)

BAKED PINEAPPLE*
or
APPLES BAKED IN FOIL
(sidebar opposite page)

*Recipes appear on opposite page.

Gingered Pork Chops and Skewered Vegetables; Garlic Toasts; Spinach Salad

GINGERED PORK CHOPS AND SKEWERED VEGETABLES

GARLIC TOASTS

Grill this delicious garlic bread while the barbecue is still heating so the coals won't be too hot. In small saucepan, combine approximately 1 cup (250 mL) butter, 8 cloves minced garlic and salt and pepper to taste. Heat over low heat until bubbly; simmer for 5 minutes. Slice 2 French bread sticks (baguettes) in half lengthwise. (Each half should be no thicker than 1 inch/2.5 cm.) Toast on grill, turning once, until golden brown. Generously brush cut side with garlic-butter mixture. Cut or break into pieces. Makes about 20 servings. Halve the recipe and use only 1 French bread stick for fewer servings.

APPLES BAKED IN FOIL

Serve baked apples with whipped cream or ice cream. To make one serving: Core 1 apple; prick in 3 or 4 places with fork. Centre apple on buttered square of heavy-duty foil large enough to wrap loosely around apple. Spoon 1 tbsp (15 mL) mincemeat into hollowed-out centre; top with 1/2 tsp (2 mL) butter. Fold up foil loosely around apple, sealing tightly. Cover and bake on grill over medium-hot coals or on medium-high setting, turning once or twice, for 25 to 40 minutes, depending on size and variety, or until apple is tender.

You'll love the sweet smoky aroma of these chops and vegetables. You can substitute cherry tomatoes or chunks of sweet red pepper for the radishes.

4	pork chops, 1 inch (2.5 cm) thick	4
8	small radishes	8
8	small mushrooms	8
8	green onions (white and light green parts)	8
8	snow peas, trimmed	8
MARINADE:		
1/2 cup	dry sherry	125 mL
1/2 cup	soy sauce	125 mL
1/4 cup	vegetable oil	50 mL
2 tbsp	maple syrup or honey	25 mL
2 tbsp	minced gingerroot	25 mL
2	cloves garlic, minced	2
2 tsp	cornstarch	10 mL
2 tsp	cold water	10 mL

• Trim and place pork chops in sturdy plastic bag set in bowl. With sharp knife, cut several small slashes in each radish and mushroom. Halve onions crosswise. Cut each snow pea crosswise into three pieces. Place vegetables in separate plastic bag.

• **Marinade:** Whisk together sherry, soy sauce, oil, maple syrup, gingerroot and garlic; pour half over meat, half over vegetables. Close bags tightly; squeeze gently to coat meat and vegetables with marinade. Refrigerate for 4 to 8 hours, turning bags occasionally. Drain marinade into small saucepan; set aside.

• Cook chops on greased grill over medium-hot coals or on medium-high setting for 8 minutes on one side.

• Meanwhile, thread mushroom, 2 onion pieces, 3 snow pea pieces and radish onto each of 8 greased metal or soaked wooden skewers; reserve marinade and add to reserved meat marinade.

• Turn pork chops and cook for 2 minutes. Add vegetables to grill; cook, turning once or twice, for about 8 minutes or until radishes are tender-crisp, removing meat when browned and no longer pink inside.

• Bring reserved marinade to boil, uncovered, over medium-high heat; boil for about 3 minutes or until reduced to 1 cup (250 mL). Blend cornstarch with water; stir into marinade; cook, stirring, for about 1-1/2 minutes or until smooth and thickened. Remove vegetables from skewers. Arrange on serving plates along with meat. Pour sauce over. Makes 4 servings.

BAKED PINEAPPLE

Place foil packages of fruit on the barbecue to cook along with the rest of the meal. (photo, p.85)

1	pineapple	1
1/4 cup	maple syrup	50 mL
2 tbsp	rum (optional)	25 mL
2 tbsp	butter	25 mL
	Whipped cream or ice cream	

• Cut off crown from pineapple and discard. Without peeling, cut pineapple lengthwise into 6 wedges. Remove core from each piece. With serrated knife, loosen pineapple from outer rind; cut fruit almost through crosswise into wedges but do not remove rind.

• Place each wedge on 12-inch (30 cm) square double sheet of foil. Drizzle with maple syrup; sprinkle with rum (if using) and dot with butter. Fold up foil, sealing loosely to leave room for steam.

• Cover and bake on grill over medium-hot coals or on medium setting for 30 to 40 minutes or until very hot and bubbly. Serve hot, topped with whipped cream or ice cream. Makes 6 servings.

Starters and Drinks

Appetizers for warm-weather dining should be light and simple to prepare, so here we offer a wide range of finger foods from easy dips for crudités to kabobs of shrimp and scallops that make great light entrées, too.

Bring soup into summer—cold, refreshing and delicious. Chill your favorite soup, set it out in an ice bucket and serve it in mugs or glass bowls at your next barbecue. And for those occasions when you want a special beverage, we have Sparkling Lemonade (p.43), Mint Iced Tea (p.45) and many other refreshing drinks.

PIZZA RUSTICA

There are as many versions of this appetizer as there are pizzas on an Italian restaurant menu. Create your own combinations with your favorite toppings.

DOUGH:

1 tsp	granulated sugar	5 mL
1 cup	warm water	250 mL
1	pkg active dry yeast (or 1 tbsp/ 15 mL)	1
2 cups	all-purpose flour	500 mL
1 cup	whole wheat flour	250 mL
1 tsp	salt	5 mL
2 tbsp	vegetable oil	25 mL

TOPPING:

1 cup	tomato sauce	250 mL
1 tsp	each dried oregano and basil	5 mL
1/4 tsp	each hot pepper flakes and coarse black pepper	1 mL
1/2 cup	sliced black olives	125 mL
1	jar (6 oz/170 mL) marinated artichoke hearts, drained and chopped	1
2 cups	shredded mozzarella cheese	500 mL
2 tbsp	freshly grated Parmesan cheese	25 mL

- **Dough:** In large bowl, dissolve sugar in water. Sprinkle yeast into water and let stand for 10 minutes or until frothy.
- Stir in 1 cup (250 mL) of the all-purpose flour, whole wheat flour and salt; beat until smooth. Blend in oil. Gradually add enough of the remaining all-purpose flour to make soft dough.
- On lightly floured surface, knead dough for about 5 minutes or until smooth and elastic. Cover with tea towel and let rest for 10 minutes.
- Lightly grease heavy-duty jelly roll pan with sides. Roll out dough into 16- x 11-inch (40 x 27.5 cm) rectangle. Transfer dough to pan.
- **Topping:** Spread tomato sauce evenly over dough. Combine oregano, basil, hot pepper flakes and black pepper. Sprinkle evenly over sauce. Scatter black olives and artichoke hearts on top. Sprinkle with mozzarella and Parmesan cheeses.
- Bake in 450°F (230°C) oven for 18 to 20 minutes or until crust is browned and filling is bubbly. Let cool for 10 minutes. Cut into squares to serve. Makes about 35 hors d'oeuvres.

Pizza Rustica; Watercress Cucumber Dip in cherry tomatoes and cucumber slices (p. 33); Smoked Salmon Wrap-Ups (p. 14); Quiche Crêpelettes (p. 30)

QUICHE CRÊPELETTES

These shells are small crêpes that are eased into tart tins and filled with a typical quiche filling. Use tiny unbaked tart shells if small crêpes are too time-consuming to make. (photo, p.29)

8	slices bacon	8
CRÊPES:		
1/2 cup	all-purpose flour	125 mL
1/2 cup	milk	125 mL
1 tsp	granulated sugar	5 mL
1	egg	1
Pinch	salt	Pinch
	Butter	
FILLING:		
1 cup	light cream	250 mL
2	eggs	2
1/2 tsp	salt	2 mL
Pinch	cayenne pepper	Pinch
1 cup	shredded Swiss cheese	250 mL
2	green onions, chopped	2

• **Crêpes:** In bowl, beat together flour, milk, sugar, egg and salt. Heat crêpe pan over medium-high heat until drop of water sizzles on surface; lightly butter skillet. Pour tablespoonful (15 mL) of batter into pan, quickly tilting pan to form free-form circle with batter; cook for about 45 seconds or until bottom is lightly browned.
• Turn crêpe over; cook for 25 seconds longer. Transfer to paper towel-lined pan. Repeat with remaining batter to make about 24 small crêpes. (Crêpes can be wrapped tightly in plastic wrap and refrigerated for up to 3 days or frozen for up to 2 months.)
• **Filling:** In bowl, beat together cream, eggs, salt and cayenne pepper; stir in cheese and onions.
• Lightly grease 2-inch (5 cm) tart tins. Fit crêpes into tart tins; spoon filling evenly into crêpes. Bake in 350°F (180°C) oven for 20 to 25 minutes or until set and browned.
• Meanwhile, in skillet, cook bacon over medium heat for about 5 minutes or until almost crisp. Cut each strip into 3 pieces; roll up each piece and secure with toothpick. To serve, remove toothpicks; top each crêpe with bacon curl. Makes 24 quiches.

TARAMA DEVILLED EGGS

Tarama (carp roe caviar) is available in jars in specialty food shops and wherever Greek or Middle Eastern groceries are sold. Tarama adds a salty but very mild fish flavor to the eggs. If tarama is unavailable, substitute golden whitefish caviar or 2 tbsp (25 mL) very finely chopped cooked ham. Halve the recipe for fewer servings. (photo, p.12)

12	hard-cooked eggs	12
1/2 cup	butter, softened	125 mL
1/4 cup	mayonnaise	50 mL
4 tsp	lemon juice	20 mL
4 tsp	tarama	20 mL
1 tbsp	finely chopped green onion	15 mL
1 tbsp	finely chopped fresh parsley	15 mL
2 tsp	Dijon mustard	10 mL
1/4 tsp	hot pepper sauce	1 mL
	Pepper	
24	small sprigs Italian parsley	24

• Halve eggs lengthwise; transfer yolks to small bowl and set aside. Cut thin sliver from bottom of each egg white so white will sit flat on serving plate.
• Mash yolks thoroughly with butter. Blend in mayonnaise, lemon juice, tarama, green onion, parsley, mustard, hot pepper sauce, and pepper to taste. Taste and adjust seasoning if necessary. Spoon into whites neatly or use pastry bag fitted with star tip. Garnish with parsley. Makes 24 eggs.

SIMPLE GARNISHES FOR APPETIZERS

• *Unpeeled apple wedges*
• *Cucumber slices or twists*
• *Fresh herbs and flowers*
• *Green onion brushes*
• *Greens such as dill, watercress or mint sprigs*
• *Lemon, lime or orange slivers, slices or zest*
• *Melon balls*
• *Parsley—curly, Italian flat-leaf, Chinese (coriander/cilantro)*
• *Green, red or yellow pepper strips*
• *Pomegranate seeds*
• *Radish slices or roses*
• *Bean or radish sprouts*
• *Sugared grapes*

Mexican Appetizer Tray

MEXICAN APPETIZER TRAY

You can present the dip in small serving dishes, but it's most impressive when layered in a deep 12-inch (30 cm) round platter. Centre the platter on a large tray and surround the dip with tortilla chips.

REFRIED BEAN LAYER:

1	can (14 oz/398 mL) refried beans	1
1/4 cup	sour cream	50 mL
1/2 tsp	chili powder	2 mL
1/2 tsp	salt	2 mL
1/4 tsp	ground cumin	1 mL

GUACAMOLE LAYER:

2	ripe avocados, peeled, pitted and chopped	2
1/3 cup	chopped onion	75 mL
1/4 cup	mayonnaise	50 mL
1 tbsp	lemon juice	15 mL
Pinch	cayenne pepper	Pinch

GARNISH:

3/4 cup	sour cream	175 mL
2 cups	shredded Cheddar or Monterey Jack cheese	500 mL
5	green onions, sliced	5
1/2 cup	sliced pitted black olives	125 mL
2	tomatoes, chopped	2
	Tortilla chips	

• **Refried Bean Layer:** Blend together refried beans, sour cream, chili powder, salt and cumin; spread over bottom of serving dish or tray.
• **Guacamole Layer:** In blender, food processor or with fork, mash avocados. Blend in onion, mayonnaise, lemon juice and cayenne. Spread over refried bean layer.
• **Garnish:** Spread sour cream over guacamole. Sprinkle cheese in ring around edge of dish. Arrange ring of green onions inside cheese, then ring of olives. Place chopped tomatoes in centre. Cover and refrigerate for up to 4 hours. Serve with tortilla chips. Makes 8 to 10 servings.

SALMON MOUSSE

Garnish this delicious appetizer with dill or parsley sprigs and lemon slices or strips of rind.

2	cans (7-1/2 oz/ 213 g) sockeye salmon	2
1/2 cup	mayonnaise	125 mL
1/4 cup	chopped fresh dill	50 mL
4 tsp	lemon juice	20 mL
1 tbsp	chopped green onion	15 mL
Dash	hot pepper sauce	Dash
2	envelopes unflavored gelatin	2
1/2 cup	water	125 mL
1 cup	whipping cream	250 mL
2	egg whites	2
1 tsp	salt	5 mL

• Drain salmon. In food processor or blender, process until smooth. There should be about 1-1/2 cups (375 mL). Transfer to saucepan. Add mayonnaise, dill, lemon juice, onion and hot pepper sauce; cook over low heat, stirring, just until mixture is warmed through.
• Meanwhile, in small saucepan, sprinkle gelatin over water; let stand for 5 minutes to soften.
• Over low heat, warm gelatin until dissolved. Stir into salmon mixture. Transfer to bowl and place in large bowl of ice and water to chill, stirring frequently, for 10 to 15 minutes or until cold and slightly thickened.
• Whip cream; set aside. In large bowl, beat egg whites with salt until stiff peaks form. Whisk about one-quarter of the beaten egg whites into salmon mixture; fold into remaining whites along with whipped cream. Pour into rinsed but not dried 6-cup (1.5 L) mould. Cover and refrigerate for at least 6 hours or up to 2 days.
• To unmould, wrap hot damp tea towel around mould for 1 minute. Using knife, loosen top edge of mousse from mould. Tilt or gently shake mould to loosen mousse. Invert rinsed serving platter on top of mould. Grasp platter and mould; quickly turn over. Shake, using quick downward motion, to release mousse from mould. Lift off mould. (If mousse sticks, repeat procedure.) Makes 6 to 8 servings.

Salmon Mousse

CRAB MOUSSE

Here's an easy variation. Substitute two cans (5 oz/142 g) crab meat for the salmon. Omit dill and add 1 tsp (5 mL) Worcestershire sauce. To prepare crab: Drain and process in food processor or blender until smooth. There should be about 1-1/2 cups (375 mL). Complete mousse as directed in recipe.

TECHNICOLOR VEGETABLE ANTIPASTO

Serve this fresh antipasto in a shallow bowl and surround it with whole wheat mini-pita breads. Halve the recipe for fewer servings. (photo, p.12)

1 lb	baby carrots	500 g
1	cauliflower (about 1 lb/500 g)	1
3/4 lb	small mushrooms	375 g
1	each large sweet red and yellow pepper	1
1	can (14 oz/398 mL) baby corncobs	1
1 cup	black olives (preferably oil-cured)	250 mL
1/4 lb	salami (preferably Genoa)	125 g
1/4 lb	Fontina cheese	125 g
1	can (7 oz/198 g) solid white tuna	1
1/4 cup	drained capers	50 mL
2	heads romaine lettuce	2
	Mini-pita breads	

DRESSING:

2 cups	olive oil	500 mL
3/4 cup	white wine vinegar	175 mL
1/3 cup	water	75 mL
2 tbsp	(approx) chopped fresh basil (or 1 tbsp/15 mL dried)	25 mL
2 tbsp	(approx) chopped chives or green onion (green part only)	25 mL
1 tbsp	salt	15 mL
2 tsp	(approx) chopped fresh oregano (or 1 tsp/5 mL dried)	10 mL
2 tsp	Dijon mustard	10 mL
1 tsp	granulated sugar	5 mL
1/2 tsp	pepper	2 mL
2	large cloves garlic, minced	2

- **Dressing:** In large saucepan, combine oil, vinegar, water, basil, chives, salt, oregano, mustard, sugar, pepper and garlic. Bring to boil over high heat; reduce heat and simmer, uncovered, for 5 minutes.
- Meanwhile, trim and pare carrots. Divide cauliflower into bite-sized florets. Trim mushrooms. Core and seed peppers; cut into 1-1/2-inch (4 cm) squares. Drain corncobs.
- Cook carrots, uncovered, in dressing for 10 minutes. Add cauliflower; cook for 10 minutes longer or until vegetables are tender-crisp. With slotted spoon, transfer to large bowl.
- In same dressing, cook mushrooms and peppers for 3 minutes; add corncobs and cook for 2 minutes longer. Transfer vegetables to bowl; let dressing cool and reserve.
- Halve and pit olives. Cut salami and cheese into 1/4-inch (5 mm) thick strips. Drain tuna; break into large chunks. Add olives, salami, cheese, tuna and capers to vegetables; toss together lightly with your hands. Cover and refrigerate until chilled.
- Separate lettuce, discarding outer leaves. Wash and dry leaves; wrap in paper towels, place in plastic bag and refrigerate.
- Just before serving, taste vegetables and adjust seasoning, adding more fresh basil, chives or oregano if desired. Add enough of reserved dressing to moisten. Line serving bowl with lettuce and fill with antipasto. Set on platter; slit pitas for easy filling and arrange around platter. Makes 20 servings.

WATERCRESS CUCUMBER DIP

Spoon this cool, creamy filling into hollowed-out cherry tomatoes or thick cucumber slices (photo, p. 29), or use as a dip for crunchy vegetable sticks. In bowl, cream together 1/2 cup (125 mL) sour cream and 1/2 cup (125 mL) cream cheese. Stir in 1/3 cup (75 mL) finely chopped peeled cucumber, 1/3 cup (75 mL) finely chopped watercress, 1 tbsp (15 mL) finely chopped green onion and 1 tbsp (15 mL) lemon juice. Season with salt and pepper to taste. Makes about 1 cup (250 mL).

BAKED GOAT CHEESE WITH WATERCRESS SAUCE

Warm chèvre with a crunchy baked coating and a refreshing green sauce makes an attractive first course.

1 cup	good-quality olive oil	250 mL
1/2 tsp	each pepper and dried basil	2 mL
1 lb	cream goat cheese (chèvre)	500 g
1 cup	fresh fine French bread crumbs	250 mL
WATERCRESS SAUCE:		
1	bunch watercress	1
2 tsp	Dijon mustard	10 mL
2	egg yolks	2
1/4 cup	red wine vinegar or sherry vinegar	50 mL
	Salt and pepper	

MAKE YOUR OWN MELBA TOAST

Remove crusts from thin slices of white or brown bread. Cut into serving-sized pieces. Spread on baking sheet and bake at 275°F (140°C), turning slices over as they brown and crisp, for about 20 minutes.

• In shallow dish, stir together oil, pepper and basil. Cut cheese into 8 rounds. (If too soft to cut into rounds, divide into 8 portions and pat into 1-inch/2.5 cm rounds.) Place in oil mixture, turning to coat all over. Refrigerate overnight, turning and basting often.

• Place bread crumbs in separate shallow dish. Place cheese rounds in crumbs, one at a time, patting on crumbs to coat cheese; reserve oil mixture. Place rounds on baking sheet. Refrigerate for at least 1 hour or up to 6 hours.

• **Watercress Sauce:** Meanwhile, remove tough stems from watercress. Measure out 2 cups (500 mL) loosely packed leaves, reserving remaining watercress in plastic bag in crisper. In food processor or blender, combine watercress, reserved oil mixture, mustard, yolks and vinegar; process for 30 seconds. Season with salt and pepper to taste; process until smooth. (Sauce can be prepared ahead, covered and refrigerated for up to 6 hours.)

• Just before serving, bake cheese in 450°F (230°C) oven for 6 to 8 minutes or until cheese begins to bubble but still holds its shape.

• Meanwhile, divide sauce among 8 salad plates; place baked cheese in centre. Garnish with reserved watercress and serve immediately. Makes 8 servings.

LEMON GRILLED SHRIMP

Garlic or dried lemon peel sprinkled on hot coals or lava rocks will add even more flavor to these delicate appetizers. Take care not to marinate the shrimp longer than indicated as they could fall apart while cooking. Serve on leaf lettuce with marinated black olives.

24	large shrimp	24
1/2 cup	lemon juice	125 mL
1/2 cup	vegetable oil	125 mL
1 tbsp	finely chopped fresh parsley	15 mL
2	cloves garlic, minced	2
2 tsp	grated lemon rind	10 mL
2 tsp	dry mustard	10 mL
1/4 tsp	cayenne pepper	1 mL
Pinch	black pepper	Pinch

• Peel shrimp, leaving on tails, and devein. Place in sturdy plastic bag set in bowl. Stir together lemon juice, oil, parsley, garlic, lemon rind, mustard, cayenne and black peppers; pour over shrimp. Close bag tightly; squeeze gently to coat shrimp well. Refrigerate for 30 minutes. Remove shrimp, reserving marinade.

• Thread each shrimp onto soaked wooden or greased metal skewer, pushing skewer through shrimp near each end but leaving centre free. (Recipe can be made ahead to this point, covered and refrigerated for up to 4 hours. Cover and refrigerate marinade separately.)

• Cook shrimp on greased grill over medium-hot coals or on medium setting, brushing often with marinade, for 2 minutes per side or until pink and firm to the touch. Makes 8 servings.

Lemon Grilled Shrimp; Baked Goat Cheese with Watercress Sauce

CHERRY TOMATOES STUFFED WITH GUACAMOLE

These colorful appetizers can be made a few hours in advance. They're particularly attractive on a cheese tray. For a special presentation, sprinkle them with red or black caviar instead of crumbled bacon. (photo, p.18)

2-1/2 cups	cherry tomatoes (about 48)	625 mL
1	large avocado	1
4 tsp	lemon juice	20 mL
1	green onion, finely chopped	1
1	clove garlic, minced	1
1/4 tsp	salt	1 mL
5	slices bacon, cooked and crumbled	5

• Using sharp knife, cut each tomato in half crosswise. Scoop out seeds; place cut sides down on paper towels. Let drain for 20 minutes.
• Meanwhile, peel and pit avocado. Place in small bowl and mash with fork. Stir in lemon juice, onion, garlic and salt; mix well. Gently spoon filling into tomato halves. Place on serving plate and cover loosely with plastic wrap; refrigerate for up to 3 hours. Just before serving, sprinkle with bacon. Makes about 96 appetizers.

MARINATED GINGER SCALLOPS

Shrimp and small chicken pieces can be substituted for the scallops in this oriental-influenced dish. For more flavor, purée the marinade ingredients. Star fruit makes an unusual and pretty garnish.

1/2 cup	olive oil	125 mL
1/4 cup	lemon juice	50 mL
2 tbsp	chopped fresh mint	25 mL
4 tsp	finely chopped gingerroot	20 mL
1-1/2 tsp	(approx) chili paste*	7 mL
1/4 tsp	salt	1 mL
3	green onions, finely chopped	3
2	cloves garlic, minced	2
1-1/2 lb	scallops	750 g

• In bowl, combine oil, lemon juice, mint, gingerroot, chili paste, salt, onions and garlic, adding more chili paste if desired. Add scallops; cover and refrigerate for 2 to 4 hours, turning to coat occasionally.
• Thread scallops onto metal or soaked wooden skewers. Cook on greased grill over medium-hot coals or on medium-high setting for 2 to 4 minutes per side or until opaque. Makes 6 servings.
*Available in specialty or oriental food shops. Or, for every 1 tsp (5 mL) chili paste, substitute 1/4 tsp (1 mL) chili powder and 5 or 6 drops hot pepper sauce, adding more if desired.

Marinated Ginger Scallops; Chilled Avocado Soup with Shrimp

CHILLED AVOCADO SOUP WITH SHRIMP

This tasty soup is fairly thick; for a thinner consistency, stir in extra chicken stock.

2	ripe avocados (about 1-1/2 lb/ 750 g total)	2
2-1/2 cups	chicken stock	625 mL
1/2 cup	buttermilk	125 mL
1 tbsp	lemon juice	15 mL
1/2 tsp	grated lemon rind	2 mL
1/4 tsp	each salt and pepper	1 mL
1	clove garlic, minced	1
GARNISH:		
1/4 lb	cooked peeled baby shrimp	125 g
	Parsley sprigs	
	Lemon wedges	

• Peel, pit and cube avocados; purée in food processor or blender. Add stock, buttermilk, lemon juice and rind, salt, pepper and garlic; process until smooth. Cover and refrigerate until chilled. Taste and adjust seasoning.

• **Garnish:** Ladle into soup bowls and garnish with shrimp and parsley. Serve with lemon. Makes 6 servings.

ALMOND SOUP WITH ORANGE ZEST

This cold soup is great for a crowd. Halve the recipe for fewer servings. Use an orange zester to make grated rind. (photo, p.12)

12 cups	chicken stock	3 L
6 cups	ground blanched almonds (2 lb/1 kg)	1.5 L
2 cups	chopped onions	500 mL
4 tsp	ground coriander	20 mL
2 cups	plain yogurt	500 mL
1 cup	each whipping cream and light cream	250 mL
GARNISH:		
3/4 cup	sliced almonds, toasted*	175 mL
1/3 cup	finely chopped chives or green onions (green part only)	75 mL
1/4 cup	coarsely grated orange rind	50 mL

• In large stockpot or saucepan, combine stock, almonds, onions and coriander. Cover and bring to boil; reduce heat and simmer for 30 to 40 minutes or until onions are very tender. Strain through large fine sieve, pressing out as much liquid as possible. Refrigerate until well chilled or for up to 2 days.
• Stir in yogurt, whipping cream and light cream. Taste and adjust seasoning if necessary.
• **Garnish:** Serve soup in chilled soup tureen. Place almonds, chives and orange rind in separate bowls. Let guests serve themselves, sprinkling garnishes over each bowl of soup. Makes 20 servings.
*Toast nuts on baking sheet in 350°F (180°C) oven for 5 minutes or until golden.

SUMMER GAZPACHO

Make this delicious chilled soup ahead of time to sip while the main course cooks. If you're in a hurry, a food processor makes quick work of this soup. Garnish it with cucumber slices.

2	avocados	2
1 cup	chopped cucumber	250 mL
1/2 cup	finely chopped green onion	125 mL
1	sweet green pepper, chopped	1
4	tomatoes, peeled, seeded and chopped	4
1 tbsp	chopped fresh parsley	15 mL
1 tbsp	lemon or lime juice	15 mL
1	clove garlic, minced	1
1 tsp	salt	5 mL
1/4 tsp	hot pepper sauce	1 mL
2 cups	tomato juice	500 mL

• Peel and pit avocados; chop into small cubes. In large bowl, combine avocados, cucumber, onion, green pepper, tomatoes, parsley, lemon juice, garlic, salt and hot pepper sauce.
• Stir in tomato juice; mix well. Refrigerate until chilled. Taste and adjust seasoning. Makes 8 servings.

Summer Gazpacho;
Chilled Cantaloupe Soup (p. 40)

CHILLED FRESH PEA AND LETTUCE SOUP

Lettuce lends a lovely sweet flavor to this soup. For a low-calorie version, substitute 1 cup (250 mL) chicken stock for the cream, sour cream or yogurt.

2 tbsp	butter	25 mL
2	leeks (white parts only), finely chopped	2
Half	head iceberg lettuce, or 1 head Boston lettuce, shredded	Half
4 cups	shelled fresh peas or frozen peas	1 L
4 cups	(approx) chicken stock	1 L
1/4 cup	chopped fresh parsley	50 mL
1 tbsp	chopped fresh tarragon (or 1 tsp/5 mL dried)	15 mL
1/2 tsp	pepper	2 mL
	Salt	
1 cup	(approx) whipping cream, sour cream or yogurt	250 mL
GARNISH:		
	Shredded lettuce	
	Chopped fresh parsley	

• In large saucepan, melt butter; add leeks and cook until tender but not browned. Stir in lettuce and cook until wilted. Add peas and mix well. Add chicken stock, parsley, tarragon, pepper, and salt to taste. Bring to boil; reduce heat, cover and cook until peas are tender, about 30 minutes.
• Purée soup in blender, food processor or food mill. Chill thoroughly. Stir in cream; taste and adjust seasoning, adding more stock or cream if desired.
• **Garnish:** Sprinkle each serving with shredded lettuce and parsley. Makes 6 to 8 servings.

CHILLED CANTALOUPE SOUP

This refreshing cold soup is particularly attractive when served in fluted cantaloupe halves with just a thin shell of cantaloupe left intact. Or serve it in a large pitcher garnished with skewered melon balls and mint sprigs. (photo, p.38)

1	large cantaloupe (or 2 small)	1
2 cups	cold water	500 mL
1	can (6 oz/170 mL) frozen orange juice concentrate	1
1/2 tsp	salt	2 mL
Pinch	mace	Pinch
2 tbsp	cornstarch	25 mL
GARNISH:		
	Sour cream	
	Mint sprigs	

• Cut cantaloupe in half and remove seeds. Using melon baller, cut pulp from one half and set balls aside.
• Remove pulp from remaining cantaloupe half and place in blender or food processor. Add any pulp left in first half; purée until smooth. (There should be 2 cups/500 mL purée.) Add 1 cup (250 mL) of the cold water, orange juice concentrate, salt and mace; process until mixed.
• In small saucepan, blend cornstarch with remaining cold water. Heat gently, stirring, until mixture thickens and becomes clear and bubbly. Stir into cantaloupe mixture. Add melon balls and refrigerate until chilled.
• **Garnish:** Ladle soup into individual bowls and garnish each serving with dollop of sour cream and mint sprig. Makes 6 servings.

CHILLED SOUPS

When you decide to serve a cold soup, remember that if it requires cooking, it needs time to cool. Allow at least three or four hours for a large bowl of soup to chill thoroughly. If you're short of time, chill the soup in several small bowls—it cools faster in small quantities.

Chill serving bowls for half an hour before serving. If you plan to have the table set with the soup in place before guests sit down, you can freeze a little of the soup in ice cube trays and add a "soup cube" to each serving.

Flavors change as soup rests, so wait until the soup is cold and cream (if called for) has been added before you adjust the seasoning. Soup also becomes thicker as it rests, so wait until it is chilled before adjusting the consistency.

Iced Cucumber Soup

ICED CUCUMBER SOUP

This refreshing low-cal soup is made without any cooking—perfect for a hot summer day. If the cucumber skin is tender, there's no need to peel it.

1	cucumber	1
	Salt	
1	small onion, chopped	1
2 tbsp	chopped fresh parsley	25 mL
1 tbsp	lemon juice	15 mL
1 cup	buttermilk	250 mL
1/2 cup	plain yogurt	125 mL
Pinch	each cumin and white pepper	Pinch
Dash	hot pepper sauce	Dash
GARNISH:		
	Plain yogurt	
	Parsley sprigs	

• Cut cucumber in half lengthwise; remove seeds. Sprinkle with salt and let stand for 30 minutes. Drain well and pat dry. Chop coarsely. In food processor or blender, process along with onion, parsley and lemon juice until almost smooth.

• In large bowl, whisk together buttermilk, 1/2 cup (125 mL) yogurt, cumin, pepper and hot pepper sauce. Stir in cucumber mixture; cover and refrigerate for at least 1 hour or until chilled. Taste and adjust seasoning if necessary.

• **Garnish:** Ladle into chilled soup bowls. Garnish with dollop of yogurt and sprig of parsley. Makes about 4 servings.

CLASSIC SANGRIA

In a large pitcher, combine 1 bottle (750 mL) dry red wine with 6 orange slices, 6 lemon slices, 2 tbsp (25 mL) each orange liqueur and brandy, and 1 tbsp (15 mL) granulated sugar. Cover and refrigerate for about 1 hour. Just before serving, add 1 bottle (750 mL) soda water and lots of ice cubes. Taste and add more sugar or soda as desired. Makes about 6 cups (1.5 L).

Summer Sangria

SUMMER SANGRIA

Instead of Sangria's classic red wine, this combination of white wine and fresh fruit is perfect for hot languid afternoons.

1/2 cup	granulated sugar	125 mL
1/2 cup	orange liqueur	125 mL
1/2 cup	brandy	125 mL
2	bottles (each 750 mL) dry white wine	2
1	(approx) bottle (750 mL) soda water, chilled	1
	Honeydew melon and cantaloupe balls	
	Lemon, lime and orange slices	
	Whole strawberries	
	Ice cubes	

• In large pitcher, combine sugar, orange liqueur, brandy and wine; cover and refrigerate for 1 to 2 hours or until chilled.
• Just before serving, stir in soda water to taste; add melon balls, lemon, lime and orange slices, strawberries and ice cubes. Makes about 12 servings.

Sparkling Lemonade

SPARKLING LEMONADE

Add bubbly soda water to old-fashioned lemonade for a refreshing treatment for an old favorite.

2 cups	cold water	500 mL
1-1/2 cups	lemon juice	375 mL
1 cup	fruit/berry sugar	250 mL
1	bottle (750 mL) soda water	1
GARNISH:		
	Thin lemon slices	
	Mint sprigs	

• In large pitcher, combine cold water, lemon juice and sugar; stir until sugar dissolves. Cover and refrigerate until chilled.

• Just before serving, gradually add soda water down edge of pitcher; stir to mix.

• **Garnish:** Pour lemonade over ice cubes in glasses. Garnish each serving with lemon slices and mint sprig. Makes about 6-1/2 cups (1.6 L).

MANGO AND YOGURT SMOOTHIE

This thick and smooth drink is also delicious made with 3 cups (750 mL) cantaloupe chunks instead of the mango.

2	mangoes (about 2-1/4 lb/1.125 kg total)	2
1/2 cup	2% plain yogurt	125 mL
1/2 cup	crushed ice	125 mL
1-1/2 cups	orange juice	375 mL
6	small stalks celery (optional)	6

• Peel and seed mangoes; cut into chunks. In blender or food processor, purée mangoes, yogurt and ice. Blend in orange juice. Pour into stemmed glasses; garnish with celery stalks (if using). Makes 6 servings.

HONEYDEW-LIME FRAPPÉ

This low-calorie drink is cool and refreshing.

1	honeydew melon (about 3 lb/1.5 kg)	1
	Juice of 1 lime	
1 cup	soda water	250 mL
	Crushed ice	
6	watermelon wedges (optional)	6

• Discard seeds from melon; remove pulp and cube. In blender, purée melon along with lime juice. Stir in soda water. Pour into glasses and add crushed ice. Garnish with watermelon wedges (if using). Makes 6 servings.

GAZPACHO COOLER

This liquid salad drink is packed with vitamins A and C.

1-1/4 cups	chopped tomatoes	300 mL
3/4 cup	coarsely chopped peeled English cucumber	175 mL
1/4 cup	chopped sweet green pepper	50 mL
2 tbsp	chopped onion	25 mL
1	clove garlic, minced	1
2 cups	tomato juice	500 mL
2 tbsp	red wine vinegar or cider vinegar	25 mL
1/4 tsp	dried dillweed	1 mL
Dash	hot pepper sauce	Dash
	Pepper	
	Alfalfa sprouts	

• In food processor or blender, process tomatoes, cucumber, green pepper, onion and garlic until smooth. Stir in tomato juice, vinegar, dillweed, hot pepper sauce, and pepper to taste. Refrigerate for at least 1 hour or until chilled. Pour into glasses; garnish with alfalfa sprouts. Makes 6 servings.

(Left to right) Honeydew-Lime Frappé; Mango and Yogurt Smoothie; Gazpacho Cooler

MINT ICED TEA

Cool and refreshing, this is delicious with any dessert. (photo, p.131)

10	tea bags	10
1/4 cup	fresh mint leaves	50 mL
6 cups	water	1.5 L
1 cup	granulated sugar	250 mL
2 cups	orange juice	500 mL
1/2 cup	lemon juice	125 mL
	Ice cubes	
GARNISH:		
	Mint sprigs	
	Lemon slices	

• In large saucepan, combine tea bags, mint and water. Bring to boil; remove from heat. Add sugar, stirring until sugar is dissolved. Cover and let steep for 30 minutes.
• Stir orange and lemon juices into steeped tea; strain and chill.
• **Garnish:** Pour mint tea into ice-filled glasses. Garnish each glass with mint sprig and lemon slice. Makes 8 cups (2 L).

VARIATION:

CRANBERRY ICED TEA:

• Prepare hot tea as above, omitting mint. Add 1 can (275 mL) frozen cranberry cocktail concentrate, along with orange and lemon juices. Chill.
• At serving time, pour into ice-filled glasses, diluting with soda water, if desired. Garnish each glass with orange slices. Makes about 8 cups (2 L).

Beef, Pork and Lamb

Beef is the traditional barbecue favorite. But don't be afraid to venture beyond tender steaks. By using marinades to tenderize, virtually any cut of beef can be barbecued. Pork today is bred to be meaty and lean. It's a meat for all occasions and there's nothing like the aroma of sizzling barbecued ribs or chops. Try the Grilled Stuffed Pork Tenderloin (p.58) for an elegant change. And don't overlook lamb for outdoor cooking. You will love our sophisticated Grilled Lamb Loins with Roasted Pepper and Garlic Sauce (p.16) and Sesame-Soy Lamb Chops (p.62).

CHUCKWAGON STEAK

Here's an easy way to use a cheaper cut of beef when you're in the mood for steak. Sprinkle soaked hickory chips on the hot coals to add to the delicious smoked flavor.

2 lb	beef chuck blade steak, 1-1/2 inches (4 cm) thick	1 kg
1/3 cup	vegetable oil	75 mL
1/3 cup	wine vinegar	75 mL
2	cloves garlic, chopped	2
2 tsp	Worcestershire sauce	10 mL
1/2 tsp	dried rosemary	2 mL
1/2 tsp	salt	2 mL
1/4 tsp	pepper	1 mL

• Place meat in plastic bag and set in large bowl. Combine oil, vinegar, garlic, Worcestershire sauce, rosemary, salt and pepper; pour over meat and close bag tightly. Marinate in refrigerator for 6 to 8 hours or overnight.

• Place 12- x 10-inch (30 x 25 cm) heavy-duty foil drip pan in centre of barbecue; fill with water. Arrange coals at back and sides of barbecue. Remove meat from marinade, reserving marinade.

• Place meat on greased grill over drip pan. Close hood and cook over medium-hot coals or on medium setting, brushing occasionally with marinade, for 18 to 20 minutes each side for medium-rare, 25 minutes on each side for medium doneness. To serve, cut diagonally into thin slices. Makes 6 servings.

HOW TO BARBECUE A STEAK
• Trim excess fat to avoid smoking and flare-ups.
• Slash fatty edges to keep meat from curling.
• Salt steaks after cooking to avoid drawing out juices.
• Turn when you notice surface bubbles on top of steak.
• Turn with tongs, never a fork, to avoid piercing meat.
• For perfectly cooked beef every time, follow this handy chart:

Thickness		Minutes per side	
	Rare	Medium	Well-done
1 inch (2.5 cm)	5 to 7	7 to 9	9 to 11
1-1/2 inches (4 cm)	7 to 9	9 to 11	15 to 18
2 inches (5 cm)	12 to 14	15 to 18	25 to 30

Chuckwagon Steak; (On barbecue) Ratatouille (p. 122); corn-on-the-cob (sidebar, p. 118)

FLANK STEAK WITH FOUR-PEPPER SALSA

This easy, economical no-fuss recipe is perfect for serving large groups of people. Be sure to slice the steaks thinly and across the grain.

4	flank steaks (about 1-1/4 lb/625 g each)	4
1 cup	dry white wine	250 mL
1/2 cup	chopped onion	125 mL
1/2 cup	olive oil	125 mL
1/4 cup	lemon juice	50 mL
2 tbsp	chopped fresh parsley	25 mL
2 tbsp	each chopped fresh oregano and thyme (or 2 tsp/10 mL dried)	25 mL
1	bay leaf	1
4	cloves garlic, minced	4
1/2 tsp	each dry mustard and pepper	2 mL
	Salt	
	Four-Pepper Salsa (recipe follows)	

• Trim excess fat from steaks and score both sides at 2-inch (5 cm) intervals; place in large shallow bowl. Combine wine, onion, oil, lemon juice, parsley, oregano, thyme, bay leaf, garlic, mustard and pepper; pour over steaks. Cover and refrigerate for at least 4 hours or overnight, turning occasionally.

• Drain steaks well, reserving marinade. Cook on greased grill over medium-hot coals or on medium-high setting, brushing often with marinade, for 4 to 6 minutes per side or until cooked to desired doneness. Transfer steaks to cutting board and let stand for 5 minutes.

• Season steaks with salt to taste; cut diagonally across the grain into thin slices. Pass Four-Pepper Salsa separately. Makes 16 to 20 servings.

FOUR-PEPPER SALSA:

1/4 cup	finely chopped green onion	50 mL
1	clove garlic, minced	1
1 cup	each diced sweet green, yellow and red pepper	250 mL
1	hot yellow pepper, finely chopped	1
1	tomato, coarsely chopped	1
2 tbsp	chopped fresh coriander	25 mL
2 tbsp	olive oil	25 mL
4 tsp	lime juice	20 mL
	Salt and pepper	

• In bowl, combine onion, garlic, green, yellow and red peppers, hot pepper, tomato, coriander, oil and lime juice; mix well. Season with salt and pepper to taste. Cover and refrigerate for 1 hour or up to 6 hours. Makes about 4-1/2 cups (1.125 L).

Flank Steak with Four-Pepper Salsa

RIB STEAKS WITH HERBED BUTTER

Prepare a log of herbed butter the night before or early in the morning and refrigerate until using.

4	rib steaks (about 1-1/2 lb/750 g total)	4
	Pepper	
HERBED BUTTER:		
1/4 cup	butter, softened	50 mL
1	small green onion, finely chopped	1
1	small clove garlic, minced	1
4 tsp	white wine (optional)	20 mL
2 tsp	finely chopped fresh parsley	10 mL
2 tsp	finely chopped fresh chervil (or 1/2 tsp/2 mL dried)	10 mL
1/4 tsp	lemon juice	1 mL

• **Herbed Butter:** In small bowl, combine butter, onion, garlic, wine (if using), parsley, chervil and lemon juice; mix well. Roll into log about 1 inch (2.5 cm) in diameter. Wrap in waxed paper and chill for several hours or overnight.

• Season steaks with pepper to taste. Cook on greased grill over hot coals or on high setting to desired doneness. Transfer to serving platter; top each steak with slice of herbed butter. Makes 4 servings.

PEACH OF A FLANK STEAK

Fresh ripe peaches, peeled and halved, can be substituted for canned. Substitute 1/2 cup (125 mL) boiling water and 2 tbsp (25 mL) granulated sugar for the peach syrup.

2	flank steaks (each 1-1/4 lb/625 g)	2
PEACH MARINADE:		
3/4 cup	port wine	175 mL
1 tbsp	lemon juice	15 mL
1	can (28 oz/796 mL) peach halves	1
MEAT MARINADE:		
1	bottle (10 oz/285 mL) chili sauce	1
1/4 cup	lemon juice	50 mL
1/4 cup	port wine	50 mL
1/4 cup	vegetable oil	50 mL
2	cloves garlic, minced	2
1 tbsp	Worcestershire sauce	15 mL
1 tbsp	Dijon mustard	15 mL
GARNISH:		
	Fresh parsley	

- Score flank steaks on each side by making diamond pattern of shallow diagonal cuts. Place in large shallow casserole or baking dish.
- **Peach Marinade:** In small bowl or plastic bag, combine port and lemon juice. Drain peaches and reserve 1/2 cup (125 mL) syrup for meat marinade. Add peaches to bowl; marinate for 2 hours or longer.
- **Meat Marinade:** In bowl, mix together chili sauce, lemon juice, wine, oil, garlic, Worcestershire sauce and mustard; stir in reserved peach syrup. Pour marinade over steaks; cover and refrigerate, turning steaks occasionally, for several hours or overnight.
- Drain steaks, reserving meat marinade. Cook on lightly greased grill over hot coals or on high setting, brushing occasionally with marinade, for 5 to 7 minutes on each side for medium-rare or until desired doneness.
- Drain peaches, reserving marinade; place peaches, cut sides up, on edge of grill to warm.
- In small saucepan, combine remaining marinades from meat and peaches. Bring to boil; remove from heat and keep warm on edge of barbecue.
- **Garnish:** To serve, cut flank steaks across the grain in thin, diagonal slices. Arrange on platter and garnish with peach halves and parsley; pass warm marinade separately. Makes 6 to 8 servings.

MUSTARD-HORSERADISH SAUCE

Here's another sauce that's wonderful served with spit-roasted prime rib of beef or any other beef dish. In small bowl, combine 1/4 cup (50 mL) dry mustard, 1 tbsp (15 mL) all-purpose flour and 1/2 tsp (2 mL) salt; stir in 2 tbsp (25 mL) prepared horseradish, 1/2 tsp (2 mL) vinegar and approximately 3 tbsp (50 mL) whipping cream to make a smooth paste. Cover and refrigerate until serving time. Makes about 1 cup (250 mL).

BEEF BARBECUE GUIDE		
Tenderness	**Cut**	**How to barbecue**
Tender	Rib roasts and steaks (including rib eye), wing, T-bone, sirloin, filet, porterhouse, strip loin, ground beef	Cook or grill on rotisserie to desired doneness. No marinating needed.
Medium-tender	Round (top, bottom and eye) roasts and steaks, sirloin tip roasts and steaks, rump roasts	Marinate before cooking to increase tenderness, although this is not essential. Grill steaks or cook roasts on rotisserie only to medium-done stage.
Medium-tender	Blade steak or roast, cross rib steak or roast	Marinate or use commercial tenderizers before cooking. Grill steaks to medium stage. If roasts are not marinated, wrap in foil and grill slowly to desired doneness. Remove foil for final 30 minutes.
Less tender	Short ribs, braising ribs, flank steak	Marinate or use commercial tenderizers before cooking. Grill short ribs slowly, brushing frequently with barbecue sauce. Grill flank steak to medium-rare stage.

BARBECUING BEEF ROASTS

- Select an evenly shaped, preferably boneless roast that has some fat covering to protect it.
- Marinate if desired.
- Season to taste but do not salt.
- See instructions below for spit-roasting and grill-roasting.
- Insert meat thermometer into centre of meat after 3/4 of cooking time has elapsed, making sure it does not touch the fat or bone. See temperatures given in chart below.
- Remove meat from grill and allow to rest for about 15 to 20 minutes before carving.

TO SPIT-ROAST:

- Balance roast on rotisserie rod, securing with tightened forks, so that meat turns with the rod.
- Cook using indirect heat over medium-hot coals or on medium-high setting.
- Place a drip pan below and slightly in front of roast. Close the lid or cover if possible.

TO GRILL-ROAST:

- Place meat on grill, centred over drip pan and close the lid.
- Cook using indirect heat over medium-hot coals or on medium-high setting.

SPIT-ROAST		ROAST GUIDELINES	GRILL-ROAST	
min. per lb	min. per kg	Internal Temp.	min. per lb	min. per kg
18 to 20	40 to 45	Rare (140°F/60°C)	15 to 20	35 to 40
22 to 25	50 to 60	Medium (160°F/70°C)	25 to 30	55 to 70
30	75	Well (170°F/75°C)	35	85

SPIT-ROASTED PRIME RIB OF BEEF WITH AIOLI SAUCE

For easy carving, ask the butcher to remove the rib bones from the meat; tie them around the roast before barbecuing for extra flavor. (photo, p.18)

5 or 6	cloves garlic, cut in half	5 or 6
11 to 12 lb	prime rib of beef, rolled and tied	5 to 6 kg
1/4 cup	butter	50 mL
2 tbsp	coarse-grained mustard	25 mL
	Pepper	
	Aioli Sauce (recipe follows)	
GARNISH (optional):		
	Tomato wedges	
	Curly endive	

- Insert garlic pieces randomly around roast between outside layer of fat and meat, making cuts only if necessary. Insert barbecue spit lengthwise through centre of roast, making sure roast is well-balanced for even turning. Combine butter with mustard; spread half the mixture over roast. Sprinkle generously with pepper to taste.
- Place spit on barbecue over drip pan; roast, basting halfway through cooking time with remaining butter mixture, at 325°F (160°C) on gas barbecue or over medium-hot coals until desired doneness or until meat thermometer registers 140°F (60°C) for rare, 145°F (65°C) for medium-rare, about 4 hours. Let stand for 10 minutes before carving.
- **Garnish:** Arrange tomatoes and endive (if using) around roast. Serve with Aioli Sauce. Makes 8 to 10 servings plus leftovers.

AIOLI SAUCE:

10	cloves garlic	10
2	egg yolks, at room temperature	2
	Juice of 1 lemon	
1 tsp	Dijon mustard	5 mL
	Salt and pepper	
1-1/2 cups	safflower oil*	375 mL

- In food processor or blender, process garlic until finely chopped. Blend in egg yolks until light in color. Add lemon juice, mustard, and salt and pepper to taste; process until mixture forms smooth paste. With motor running, gradually pour in oil in slow steady stream. Blend until sauce is thickened and shiny. Transfer to serving bowl; cover with plastic wrap and refrigerate until serving time. Makes about 1-1/2 cups (375 mL).
*Use half olive oil, if desired.

SMOKED BONELESS BEEF

If you prefer, use a dry cure or brine with your favorite herbs instead of the marinade suggested here. Using wood chips for at least two hours during the cooking time will further enhance the smoky flavor.

1	sirloin tip or rolled top round roast of beef (about 5 lb/ 2.2 kg)	1
	Boiling water	
MARINADE:		
1/2 cup	vegetable oil	125 mL
1/2 cup	mango chutney	125 mL
1/4 cup	lemon or lime juice	50 mL
2	cloves garlic, crushed	2

- **Marinade:** Combine oil, chutney, lemon juice and garlic; pour into large plastic bag.
- Place meat in marinade; press out air and seal with twist tie. Place in large bowl and refrigerate overnight, turning bag several times.
- Remove meat from marinade; pour marinade into water pan set over hot coals and soaked wood chips.
- Pour in enough boiling water to half-fill water pan. Place meat on rack above water pan; cover smoker and smoke-cook for 6 to 7 hours or until meat thermometer registers desired doneness and meat is tender. Makes about 12 servings plus leftovers.

SMOKE COOKING

Smoke cookers cook food with very low heat while surrounding it with moist, steamy smoke. Soaked wood chips on the heat source and seasonings in the water pan combine to impart a distinctive flavor to meats, poultry and seafood. (For diagram, see p. 151)

Although smoking food at home does not preserve it as old-style smokehouses do, it gives your cuts of meat a wonderful flavor. You can enhance the flavor even more by curing the food before you smoke-cook it.

The heat of the fuel, the temperature outdoors, the wind and the density of the food will all affect the cooking time. Experiment with your smoke cooker. You should be less rigid with this style of cooking as timing is not exact.

Here are some tips on using your smoke cooker and we've included a variety of recipes (Smoked Boneless Beef p. 52; Smoked Pork Loin p. 60; Smoked Lamb Chops p. 65; Smoked Turkey p. 81; and Smoked Whole Trout p. 84) for you to enjoy.

CURING YOUR FOOD

There are two ways to cure: Dry Cure—a mixture of coarse salt (sea or pickling salt), sugar and seasonings which is rubbed over the food.
Wet Cure (Brine)—coarse salt and sugar dissolved in water and seasoned with herbs and spices in which the food is marinated.

1. Place food to be cured in glass, crockery or plastic containers (never wood or metal), rub with dry cure or marinate in wet cure, wrap with plastic and refrigerate for several hours or overnight.
2. Rinse cured food under cold running water, place on wire rack and let dry at room temperature for 1 to 2 hours before smoking. Food is dry when surface becomes glossy.

TO SMOKE-COOK

1. Start Fire:
While the temperature on gas smoke cookers is easy to control, charcoal-fuelled smoke cookers are a bit more difficult. Space the briquettes far enough apart so the temperature on the rack never rises above 200°F (100°C). *The smoker should never become so hot that you can't place your hands on top of the cooker.* You may need to add several briquettes during smoking to maintain the temperature. Never use charcoal that has been impregnated with starter fluid.

2. Add Flavor Enhancers to Fire:
Place wood chips that have been soaked in water for at least 30 minutes on top of the heat source. Hickory, oak and mesquite are the most popular wood chips; cherry, apple and other fruitwoods can also be used. Never use pine or fir with resin. To enhance the smoky flavor further, replenish chips during smoke-cooking. You will need four to six chips to smoke-cook a large roast, turkey or whole fish.

Other flavor enhancers, such as fresh gingerroot, dry chilies, bay leaves, garlic cloves, fresh herbs and citrus rinds, can also be soaked in water for 30 minutes and placed on top of the heat source along with the wood chips.

Instead of using wood chips, you can add liquid smoke directly to the food or marinade to produce a smoky flavor. It is very concentrated and should be used sparingly.

3. Fill Water Pan:
Fill the water pan above the heat source with warmed fruit juice, stock, beer, or marinade combined with water to enhance the flavor of food. Add more liquid to the pan once or twice during the smoking of large pieces of food; a sizzling or frying sound warns you when the pan has boiled dry.

4. Start Cooking:
Place the food on the grilling rack above the water pan, cover and smoke-cook for the recommended time. Use a meat thermometer for greater accuracy.

Smoke-cooked food should be handled like any freshly cooked food. Enjoy the same day or refrigerate for several days.

Smoked Boneless Beef

SESAME SHORT RIBS

Beef short ribs should always be precooked before grilling to tenderize the meat and reduce the fat.

3 lb	beef short ribs	1.5 kg
1 cup	water	250 mL
1/2 cup	soy sauce	125 mL
1/4 cup	packed brown sugar	50 mL
2 tbsp	chopped gingerroot (or 1 tsp/5 mL ground ginger)	25 mL
1	clove garlic, minced	1
2 tbsp	liquid honey	25 mL
1 tbsp	sesame oil	15 mL
2 tbsp	sesame seeds	25 mL

• In large saucepan, combine ribs, water, soy sauce, sugar, gingerroot and garlic; bring to boil. Reduce heat, cover and simmer for about 1 hour or until ribs are tender, turning occasionally. With slotted spoon, transfer ribs to platter; set aside.

• To saucepan, add honey and sesame oil; bring to boil and cook for 10 to 15 minutes or until sauce is reduced to 1 cup (250 mL).

• Cook ribs on lightly greased grill over hot coals or high setting, turning and basting occasionally with reduced sauce, for 10 to 15 minutes or until glazed and browned. Transfer ribs to serving platter.

• Meanwhile, in small skillet, toast sesame seeds over medium-high heat, stirring often, for 3 to 5 minutes or until golden. Sprinkle over ribs. Makes about 4 servings.

SPICY SPARERIBS

Ribs are always a popular barbecue choice. Simmer the ribs early in the day and then pop them into thick tangy sauce to marinate. It takes only about 20 minutes on the barbecue to finish cooking the ribs to tender perfection.

4-1/2 lb	spareribs	2.25 kg
1/2 tsp	chopped fresh thyme (or 1/2 tsp/2 mL crumbled dried)	2 mL
1/4 tsp	salt	1 mL
1/4 tsp	pepper	1 mL
1	small bay leaf	1
Half	stalk celery, chopped	Half
Half	onion, chopped	Half
SAUCE:		
1/2 cup	strong coffee	125 mL
1/2 cup	ketchup	125 mL
1/4 cup	packed brown sugar	50 mL
3 tbsp	cider vinegar	50 mL
2 tbsp	butter	25 mL
1-1/2 tsp	Worcestershire sauce	7 mL
1/2 tsp	grated lemon rind	2 mL
1 tbsp	lemon juice	15 mL

• In large saucepan or stock pot, cover ribs with cold water; add thyme, salt, pepper, bay leaf, celery and onion. Bring to gentle boil; cover, reduce heat and simmer for about 45 minutes or until ribs are tender. Remove ribs and place in shallow glass dish. Set aside. (Strain cooking liquid and refrigerate to use as soup stock.)

• **Sauce:** In small saucepan, combine coffee, ketchup, sugar, vinegar, butter, Worcestershire, lemon rind and juice. Bring to gentle boil; reduce heat and simmer for 15 minutes to blend flavors. Let cool.

• Cut strips of ribs into serving portions of 2 or 3 ribs. Pour sauce all over ribs in dish and marinate for 3 to 4 hours in refrigerator or for 30 minutes at room temperature.

• Remove ribs from sauce, reserving any remaining sauce. Cook ribs on greased grill over medium-hot coals or on medium setting, turning and brushing occasionally with reserved sauce, for about 20 minutes or until meat is browned and edges are crisped.

• Arrange on large wooden board or platter and serve immediately. Makes 8 to 10 servings.

Spicy Spareribs; Garlic Toasts (sidebar, p. 27); Barbecued Beans (p. 118)

TEX-MEX BARBECUED PORK BUTT

Grilled pork is always delicious. Here it takes on an extra flavor dimension with a spicy Mexican-style marinade. Use an inexpensive cut of meat to butterfly for this tantalizing barbecue.

3-3/4 lb	boneless pork butt	1.7 kg
MARINADE:		
2 tbsp	vegetable oil	25 mL
3/4 cup	finely chopped onions	175 mL
1	clove garlic, minced	1
2	jalapeño peppers, slivered (2 tbsp/25 mL)*	2
1/2 cup	tomato sauce	125 mL
1 tbsp	white vinegar	15 mL
1 tbsp	Worcestershire sauce	15 mL
1 tsp	chili powder	5 mL
1/2 tsp	each salt, paprika, ground cumin and dried oregano	2 mL
1/4 tsp	each black pepper and cayenne pepper	1 mL

- **Marinade:** In heavy saucepan, heat oil over low heat; fry onions, garlic and jalapeño peppers for 3 to 5 minutes or until onions are translucent. Stir in tomato sauce, vinegar, Worcestershire sauce, chili powder, salt, paprika, cumin, oregano, black and cayenne peppers. Bring to boil, cover, reduce heat and simmer for 10 minutes or until flavors have blended. Let cool completely.
- Meanwhile, trim fat from outside of pork. To butterfly, use sharp knife held parallel to work surface and slice meat in half lengthwise almost through to other long side, leaving 1/2 inch (1 cm) intact. Open up like a book; score top of meat with 1/2-inch (1 cm) deep slashes, making 3 slashes lengthwise and 5 crosswise.
- Place meat in large glass dish; spread marinade over. Cover and marinate for 4 hours at room temperature or overnight in refrigerator. Remove from refrigerator about 1 hour before barbecuing to bring to room temperature.
- Remove meat, reserving any marinade. Cook, scored side down, on greased grill over medium-hot coals or on medium setting for 40 minutes, basting often with reserved marinade. Turn meat over and cook, basting often with marinade, for 40 minutes longer or until temperature on meat thermometer reaches 170°F (75°C), meat is firm and juices run clear when meat is pierced.
- Transfer meat to cutting board and let stand for 5 to 10 minutes before carving crosswise into thin slices. Makes 6 to 8 servings.

*If using canned peppers, rinse before cutting into slivers.

CHINESE BARBECUED RIBS

These moist flavorful ribs are cooked first, then glazed on the grill with a sweet-and-sour barbecue sauce.

6 lb	spareribs	3 kg
1 cup	ketchup	250 mL
1/2 cup	soy sauce	125 mL
1/4 cup	lemon or lime juice	50 mL
1/4 cup	rice vinegar* or half white vinegar, half water	50 mL
1/4 cup	hoisin sauce* (optional)	50 mL
2	cloves garlic, minced	2
2 tsp	cornstarch	10 mL
1/2 cup	liquid honey	125 mL

- In large pot, cover ribs with water; simmer, covered, for about 1 hour or just until tender. Drain and arrange in shallow pan. (Alternatively, microwave 3 lb/1.5 kg at a time, in covered shallow dish, at Medium/50% for about 20 minutes, turning halfway through.) Mix together ketchup, soy sauce, lemon juice, vinegar, hoisin sauce, garlic and cornstarch; stir until cornstarch is dissolved. Pour over ribs; marinate in refrigerator for at least 2 hours.
- Remove ribs, reserving marinade. Cook on grill over medium-hot coals or on medium setting for 10 minutes, turning once and brushing often with marinade. Add honey to remaining marinade and brush over ribs; cook, turning once or twice and brushing with honey mixture, for about 10 minutes or until richly glazed. Cut ribs into serving-sized pieces of one or two ribs each. Makes about 6 servings.

*Available in specialty shops and many supermarkets.

TENDERIZING TIPS

Economical cuts of meat can be just as tasty as the more expensive ones. Marinating meat is an easy way to tenderize inexpensive cuts that often have tough connective tissues (see Marinades and Sauces, pages 92–99). The acid in a marinade (wine, lemon juice or vinegar) will soften tough connective tissues.

There's a trick to cutting and carving less tender meat, too. Always cut large pieces of meat across the grain into thin slices.

The third secret is to keep the juices inside the meat when grilling. Use long-handled tongs to turn the meat so that you don't pierce the surface and lose these flavorful juices.

PECAN-STUFFED PORK CHOPS

Pecans add unique flavor to these pork chops.

1/4 cup	finely chopped pecans	50 mL
2 tbsp	fine fresh bread crumbs	25 mL
2 tbsp	butter, melted	25 mL
1 tsp	each fresh basil and thyme (or 1/4 tsp/1 mL each dried)	5 mL
1/4 tsp	pepper	1 mL
4	boneless pork chops, 3/4-inch (2 cm) thick (about 1 lb/500 g total)	4
2 tbsp	Dijon mustard	25 mL
1 tbsp	vegetable oil	15 mL

• Combine pecans, bread crumbs, butter, basil, thyme and pepper; mix well and set aside.

• Trim all but 1/4 inch (5 mm) fat from pork chops. With sharp knife, insert tip into fat side of each chop and cut pocket inside chop, leaving 1/2-inch (1 cm) opening. Evenly divide pecan mixture and stuff into each chop; press opening closed.

• Combine mustard with oil; brush half of the mixture over chops and set remaining mixture aside.

• Cook chops on greased grill over medium-hot coals or on medium setting for 12 to 15 minutes or until pork is no longer pink inside, turning once and brushing with remaining mustard mixture. Makes 4 servings.

CITRUS SUNSHINE PORK CHOPS

Serve these tangy orange- and lemon-flavored chops with sweet potato slices cooked in foil on the grill. Round out the meal with fresh green peas and a salad of leaf lettuce and radishes.

4	pork chops (about 1-1/2 lb/750 g total)	4
1 tsp	each grated orange and lemon rind	5 mL
1/4 cup	orange juice	50 mL
2 tbsp	lemon juice	25 mL
2 tbsp	vegetable oil	25 mL
2 tbsp	minced fresh chives or green onions	25 mL
3/4 tsp	chili powder	4 mL
1/4 tsp	each paprika and pepper	1 mL
1/4 tsp	hot pepper sauce	1 mL
	Salt	

• Trim all but 1/4 inch (5 mm) fat from chops; nick fat on chops at 1-inch (2.5 cm) intervals.

• In shallow dish large enough to hold chops in single layer, mix together orange and lemon rind, orange and lemon juices, oil, chives, chili powder, paprika, pepper and hot pepper sauce. Add chops, turning to coat both sides; cover and marinate in refrigerator for at least 1 hour or up to 1 day.

• Remove chops, reserving any marinade; cook chops on greased grill over medium-hot coals or on medium-high setting, turning once and brushing with marinade, for 12 to 15 minutes or until no longer pink inside. Season with salt to taste. Makes 4 servings.

BARBECUING PORK

• The secret to perfect barbecued pork is to cook it over low to moderate heat. You should be able to hold your hand over the grill for 4 seconds for medium heat, 5 to 6 seconds for low heat. Anything less is too hot for pork.

• Select pork steaks that are 1 to 1-1/4 inches (2.5 to 3 cm) thick.

• Bring meat to room temperature before placing on grill.

• Do not overcook or pork becomes dry and less tender. Cook only until meat has lost its pinkness in centre.

Maple-Glazed Ribs

MAPLE-GLAZED RIBS

*The mellow flavor of maple is an ideal
enhancement for meaty back ribs.*

3 lb	pork back ribs	1.5 kg
3/4 cup	maple syrup	175 mL
2 tbsp	packed brown sugar	25 mL
2 tbsp	ketchup	25 mL
1 tbsp	cider vinegar	15 mL
1 tbsp	Worcestershire sauce	15 mL
1/2 tsp	salt	2 mL
1/2 tsp	dry mustard	2 mL

• In large pot, cover ribs with water; simmer, covered, for about 1 hour or until tender. (Alternatively, microwave, in covered shallow dish, at Medium/50% for about 20 minutes, turning halfway through.)
• In small saucepan, combine maple syrup, sugar, ketchup, vinegar, Worcestershire sauce, salt and mustard; bring to boil. Pour over ribs; marinate in refrigerator for about 2 hours.
• Remove ribs, reserving marinade. Cook over medium-hot coals or on medium setting, turning occasionally and brushing with sauce, for about 20 minutes or until tender and glazed. Cut into serving-sized pieces. Makes about 4 to 6 servings.

Grilled Stuffed Pork Tenderloin; Cherry Tomatoes with Fresh Basil; Sliced Potatoes and Red Onions

GRILLED STUFFED PORK TENDERLOIN

Lean, tender pork rolled around a mushroom-herb stuffing will be the highlight of any summer menu.

2	pork tenderloins (about 1-1/2 lb/ 750 g each)	2
2 tsp	butter	10 mL
2 tbsp	chopped onion	25 mL
1	small clove garlic, chopped	1
1 tbsp	pine nuts	15 mL
3/4 cup	chopped mushrooms	175 mL
1/2 cup	fresh bread crumbs	125 mL
1 tbsp	chopped fresh parsley	15 mL
1 tbsp	chopped fresh sage	15 mL
	Salt and pepper	
2 tbsp	olive oil	25 mL
2 tbsp	apple cider or apple juice	25 mL

• Butterfly pork tenderloins by splitting each horizontally in half, leaving 1/4 inch (5 mm) intact along other long side. Open up like book and pound to flatten slightly. Set aside.
• In skillet, melt butter over medium-high heat; sauté onion, garlic and pine nuts for about 2 minutes or until onion is softened. Add mushrooms; cook for 3 to 5 minutes or until softened.
• Transfer to bowl and add bread crumbs, parsley and sage. Season with salt and pepper to taste; mix well. Spread stuffing over tenderloins, leaving border all around. Fold each in half lengthwise and secure with greased skewers.
• In small bowl, whisk together oil and apple cider for basting. Cook tenderloins on greased grill over hot coals or on medium-high setting, turning and brushing occasionally with cider mixture, for 30 minutes or until pork is no longer pink inside. Makes 4 servings.

SLICED POTATOES AND RED ONIONS

Cook packages of herbed and buttered vegetables alongside the main dish for a quick and easy taste of summer. This combination is perfect with Grilled Stuffed Pork Tenderloin (recipe this page). On 4 greased large pieces of foil, alternately layer 4 sliced new potatoes and 4 sliced red onions. Sprinkle 1 tbsp (15 mL) parsley over each. Fold up foil around vegetables and seal tightly to form packets. Place on greased grill over hot coals or on medium-high setting and cook for about 30 minutes or until potatoes are tender. Makes 4 servings.

GLAZED LOIN OF PORK WITH MELON AND CHEESE SAUCE

Whether the meat is cooked on a spit or in a covered barbecue, it must be done but not overdone. To test for doneness, insert a meat thermometer into the thickest part of the meat. A long narrow roast cooks faster than a short wide roast.

6 lb	boneless pork loin roast	3 kg
1	cantaloupe, peeled and cut in wedges	1
GLAZE:		
1/2 cup	orange juice	125 mL
1/4 cup	honey	50 mL
1 tbsp	lemon juice	15 mL
1 tsp	cornstarch	5 mL
1/2 tsp	celery seeds	2 mL
CHEESE SAUCE:		
1/2 lb	cream cheese, softened	250 g
1/4 cup	whipping cream	50 mL
1 tbsp	chopped fresh chives	15 mL

• Centre roast on greased spit and place over drip pan in front of coals. (Alternatively, place on greased grill over drip pan and cover with hood.) Spit-roast, rotating constantly, or cook over hot coals or on high setting for 1-1/2 to 2 hours or until meat thermometer registers 175°F (80°C).

• **Glaze.** Meanwhile, in saucepan, combine orange juice, honey, lemon juice, cornstarch and celery seeds; bring to boil and cook until thickened slightly. Brush over roast several times during last 30 minutes of cooking. Let roast stand for 10 minutes before carving.

• Meanwhile, heat cantaloupe wedges on edge of grill.

• **Cheese Sauce:** Cream together cheese and cream; mix in chives.

• Slice pork thickly and serve on cantaloupe wedges. Spoon cheese sauce over top. Makes 8 servings.

CHERRY TOMATOES WITH FRESH BASIL

Garden-fresh tomatoes sprinkled with fresh basil make a simple and delicious accompaniment to any meal. Divide 2 cups (500 mL) cherry tomatoes among 4 greased pieces of foil; sprinkle 1 tbsp (15 mL) chopped fresh basil evenly over each. Fold up foil loosely around tomatoes and seal tightly to form packets. Place on greased grill over hot coals or on medium-high setting and cook for 5 to 10 minutes or until heated through. Makes 4 servings.

SMOKED PORK RIBS

One whiff of the tantalizing aroma of these ribs will set taste buds tingling. The slow cooking over soaked hickory chips you add to the hot coals gives them a deliciously different flavor.

2 tbsp	vegetable oil	25 mL
1	onion, chopped	1
3/4 cup	ketchup	175 mL
1/2 cup	apple juice	125 mL
1/4 cup	molasses	50 mL
1-1/2 tsp	salt	7 mL
1/2 tsp	dry mustard	2 mL
4 lb	pork back ribs	2 kg

• In small saucepan, heat oil over medium-high heat; cook onion until tender but not browned. Blend in ketchup, apple juice, molasses, salt and mustard; bring to boil, remove from heat and set aside.

• Place heavy-duty foil drip pan in centre of barbecue; fill with water. Arrange coals around sides of barbecue. Place ribs on greased grill over drip pan. Close hood and cook over low heat or on low setting for 40 minutes on each side. Baste both sides of ribs with sauce; cook, uncovered, turning and basting occasionally with sauce, for 20 minutes longer. Serve with remaining sauce. Makes 4 to 6 servings.

SKEWERS OF PORK WITH ZUCCHINI AND GREEN ONIONS

Serve this lean and tender pork kabob on a bed of rice, garnished with peach chutney and a side dish of baby carrots.

2 tbsp	vegetable oil	25 mL
2 tbsp	lemon juice	25 mL
1 tbsp	white wine vinegar	15 mL
1 tsp	curry powder	5 mL
1	clove garlic, minced	1
1-1/4 lb	lean boneless pork	625 g
8	green onions	8
1	zucchini	1
	Salt	

• In shallow bowl, stir together oil, lemon juice, vinegar, curry powder and garlic. Cut pork into 1-inch (2.5 cm) cubes. Cut onions into 1-inch (2.5 cm) lengths. Cut zucchini into 1/2-inch (1 cm) thick slices. Add pork, onions and zucchini to curry marinade, tossing to coat thoroughly. Cover and marinate in refrigerator for up to 8 hours.
• Thread pork loosely onto greased metal or soaked wooden skewers, alternating with onions threaded crosswise, and zucchini. Cook over medium-hot coals or on medium-high setting, turning occasionally, until meat is browned but no longer pink inside, about 15 minutes. Season with salt to taste. Makes 4 servings.

SMOKED PORK LOIN

If you are concerned about undercooking pork and do not have a meat thermometer, remove the roast from the smoker after 6 hours (See Smoke Cooking, p. 52) and roast it in a 325°F (160°C) oven for one hour longer or until meat thermometer registers 175°F (80°C).

1	boneless rolled pork loin (about 5 lb/2.5 kg)	1
1 or 2	cloves garlic, slivered	1 or 2
1 tsp	celery seeds	5 mL
1 tbsp	each chopped fresh sage and basil	15 mL
	Pepper	
1 cup	barbecue sauce*	250 mL
	Boiling water	

• Make small slits in top of meat; insert garlic. Combine celery seeds, sage, basil, and pepper to taste; sprinkle over meat.
• In small saucepan, bring barbecue sauce to boil. Pour into water pan set over hot coals and soaked wood chips; pour in enough boiling water to fill pan two-thirds full.
• Place meat on rack above water pan; cover smoker and smoke-cook for about 6 hours or until meat thermometer registers 175°F (80°C). Makes about 12 generous servings.
* Use your favorite barbecue sauce or see pages 95–99.

If you're purchasing skewers, look for flat metal ones that are narrow and well-pointed. Sharp, slender skewers will not break fragile food like mushrooms. The length you choose should be suitable for the size of your barbecue. Only short ones will fit onto a narrow hibachi, but you can always use two per serving.

Wooden skewers are sharp and handy for appetizer, fruit or vegetable kabobs. Before each use, soak them in water for 30 minutes or they will char and disappear in flames while your food cooks.

Serve food to your family and guests right on the skewers. Diners can easily use a fork to push everything off onto a plate or a bed of steaming rice, bulgur or refreshing greens like herbs and watercress. Or, each guest can slip the skewer into the hollow opening of warm pita bread and pull its contents off to make a neat little package. Since no cutlery is needed, this is a good way to serve kabobs on picnics.

Mixed Grill Kabobs

MIXED GRILL KABOBS

Mix and match meats and vegetables to make stunning barbecued kabobs that will please everyone's palate. You can use trimmed lamb loin chops and cubed sirloin steak, bundles of green beans and asparagus tied with blanched green onions, leeks, red onion, oyster mushrooms, baby summer squash and sweet red and yellow peppers.

4	lamb loin chops, trimmed	4
1/2 lb	sirloin steak, cut in 1-1/2-inch (4 cm) cubes	250 g
2 cups	vegetable chunks*	500 mL
MARINADE:		
1/3 cup	olive oil	75 mL
1/4 cup	red wine vinegar	50 mL
1	clove garlic, minced	1
2 tbsp	chopped fresh basil (or 2 tsp/10 mL dried)	25 mL
1 tbsp	chopped fresh rosemary (or 1 tsp/ 5 mL dried)	15 mL
1 tbsp	dry sherry	15 mL
1/4 tsp	pepper	1 mL

• Place lamb and sirloin steak in large bowl.
• **Marinade:** Whisk together oil, vinegar, garlic, basil, rosemary, sherry and pepper; pour over meat. Marinate at room temperature for 1 hour; drain, reserving marinade.
• Thread meat and vegetables onto 4 greased metal or soaked wooden skewers. Brush with some of the marinade. Cook on lightly greased grill over hot coals or on high setting, turning occasionally and brushing with marinade, for 6 to 8 minutes or until meat is desired doneness and vegetables are tender-crisp. Makes 4 servings.
*If using leeks, onions, baby potatoes, summer squash or carrots, microwave at High for 1 minute or blanch in boiling water before cooking.

SESAME-SOY LAMB CHOPS

Brush some of the marinade over halved eggplant and zucchini for extra flavor. If desired, substitute 1 tbsp (15 mL) sesame oil for the same amount of vegetable oil for additional flavor.

8	lamb loin chops	8
1/4 cup	vegetable oil	50 mL
1/4 cup	soy sauce	50 mL
1 tbsp	chopped gingerroot	15 mL
1 tbsp	lemon juice	15 mL
16	sprigs fresh rosemary	16
1/3 cup	sesame seeds	75 mL

• Place lamb in heavy plastic bag and set in shallow dish. Mix together oil, soy sauce, gingerroot and lemon juice. Pour over lamb; seal bag tightly. Refrigerate for at least 1 hour or up to 4 hours, turning bag occasionally. Soak rosemary sprigs in water for 30 minutes.
• Spread sesame seeds on waxed paper. Drain lamb and dredge with sesame seeds.
• Cook lamb on greased grill over medium-hot coals or on medium setting, turning once, for 10 to 15 minutes or until desired doneness. Place half of the rosemary on lamb while grilling; add remaining sprigs when lamb is turned over. Makes 4 servings.

GRILLED LEMON-GARLIC LEG OF LAMB

Combine rosemary, garlic and lemon juice in a flavorful marinade for grilled or broiled lamb.

3	cloves garlic, minced	3
2 tbsp	lemon juice	25 mL
1/2 tsp	grated lemon rind	2 mL
1/2 tsp	dried rosemary (or 1 tbsp/15 mL chopped fresh)	2 mL
1/4 tsp	pepper	1 mL
1/4 cup	olive or vegetable oil	50 mL
1	boned butterflied leg of lamb (about 3 lb/1.5 kg)	1

• In small bowl or food processor, mix together garlic, lemon juice and rind, rosemary and pepper; gradually pour in oil and mix until combined.
• Place lamb in shallow dish; pour marinade over, turning to coat both sides. Cover and let stand at room temperature for 1 to 2 hours or refrigerate overnight (bring to room temperature before cooking).
• Remove lamb from marinade reserving marinade. Cook lamb on greased grill over hot coals or on high setting for 15 minutes, brushing with marinade several times; turn and cook for 12 minutes longer or until meat is pink inside.
• Let meat stand for 10 minutes before slicing thinly across the grain to serve. Makes 6 to 8 servings.

BARBECUING LAMB LEGS AND RACKS

• Always use a meat thermometer. Overcooking dries lamb out. Internal temperatures for whole or butterflied leg of lamb should be 140°F (60°C) for rare, 150°F (65°C) for medium and 160°F (70°C) for well-done.

• Let lamb leg stand, loosely covered with foil, for 10 minutes before carving.
• To barbecue lamb racks: Place racks, bone side down, on greased grill over medium-hot coals or on medium-high setting and cook for about 12 minutes. Turn racks and cook about 8 minutes

longer for rare lamb. Allow 5 to 10 more minutes for medium or well-done. To test for doneness, press meat lightly with fingers protected by paper towels. If it is softly springy to the touch, it's rare; if it's very firm; it's well-done. The lamb will be nicer if rare. Cut between ribs to serve.

Sesame-Soy Lamb Chops; grilled vegetables

ROSEMARY MUSTARD LAMB CHOPS

Succulent lamb chops sealed with a rosemary mustard coating highlight a summer supper menu.

12	lamb loin chops	12
	Salt and pepper	
1/2 cup	Dijon mustard	125 mL
2 tsp	crushed dried rosemary	10 mL

• Pat chops dry with paper towel; sprinkle with salt and pepper to taste. Combine mustard with rosemary; brush 1 tsp (5 mL) over one side of each chop. Cook over hot coals or on medium-high setting, mustard sides down, for 4 minutes.
• Brush evenly with remaining mustard mixture. Turn chops over and cook for 4 minutes longer or until desired doneness. Makes 4 servings.

TRICOLOR PEPPER PACKET

Here's a colorful mixture of vegetables steamed in a foil packet. On each of 4 greased 24- x 12-inch (60 x 30 cm) pieces of foil, divide 1 each thinly sliced large sweet green, yellow and red pepper and 1 thinly sliced onion. Sprinkle with salt and pepper to taste. Fold up foil around vegetables and seal tightly to form packet. Place on greased grill over hot coals or on medium-high setting; cook for 15 minutes or until vegetables are tender. Makes 4 servings.

SMOKED LAMB CHOPS

Choose thick, well-trimmed lamb chops for long, slow cooking in a smoker (See Smoke Cooking, p. 52). Add soaked wood chips, preferably apple or cherry, for a different flavor.

12	loin lamb chops (3 lb/1.5 kg)	12
	Boiling water	
MARINADE:		
1 cup	vermouth or chicken stock	250 mL
1/4 cup	vegetable oil	50 mL
3	cloves garlic, crushed	3
1/4 cup	fresh rosemary	50 mL
1 tsp	salt	5 mL

• Place chops in shallow glass or plastic dish; set aside.

• **Marinade:** In bowl, blend together vermouth, oil, garlic, rosemary and salt; pour over chops, cover with plastic wrap and refrigerate for at least 4 hours or overnight.

• Remove chops from marinade; pour marinade into water pan set over hot coals and soaked wood chips. Pour in enough boiling water to half-fill water pan.

• Place chops on rack above water pan; cover smoker and smoke-cook for 2-1/2 to 3 hours or until meat thermometer registers desired doneness. Makes 6 servings.

GRILLED LAMB SHOULDER PROVENÇALE

Perfect for inexpensive entertaining on a budget, lamb shoulder will taste even better when marinated with the herbs of Provence—rosemary, thyme and basil.

1	boneless shoulder of lamb (about 2 lb/1 kg)	1
MARINADE:		
1/3 cup	olive or vegetable oil	75 mL
1/3 cup	lemon juice	75 mL
1/3 cup	white wine	75 mL
2 tbsp	finely chopped onion	25 mL
2 tbsp	chopped fresh parsley	25 mL
1	clove garlic, minced	1
1	bay leaf	1
1/2 tsp	each dried rosemary, thyme and basil	2 mL
1/2 tsp	salt	2 mL
	Pepper	

• With sharp knife, slice horizontally through lamb, stopping about 1 inch (2.5 cm) from opposite edge. Open meat like a book; flatten with flat of knife. Trim membrane and any excess fat. Place lamb in heavy plastic bag and set in shallow dish.

• **Marinade:** In bowl, combine oil, lemon juice, wine, onion, parsley, garlic, bay leaf, rosemary, thyme, basil, salt, and pepper to taste. Pour over lamb in plastic bag; press air out of bag and secure with twist tie. Marinate for at least 4 hours or overnight in refrigerator. Remove lamb from marinade, reserving marinade.

• Cook lamb flat on lightly greased grill over hot coals or on high setting, turning once and basting often with reserved marinade, for about 20 minutes or until desired doneness.

• To serve, slice lamb across the grain into 1/2-inch (1 cm) thick slices. Makes about 6 servings.

Rosemary Mustard Lamb Chops; Tricolor Pepper Packet; New Potatoes in Garlic-Basil Butter (sidebar, p. 124)

Burgers and Hotdogs

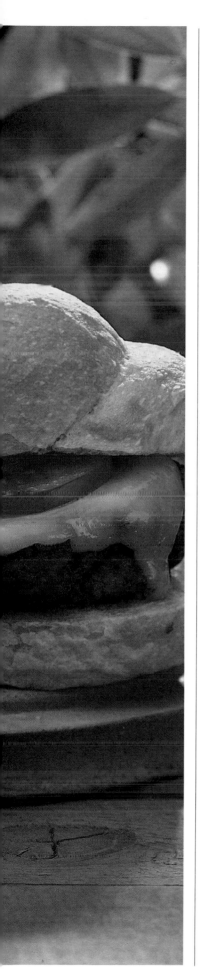

The big attraction of a burger or hotdog supper is that all you need to complete the meal is a salad. Make burgers classic with beef, try them tasty with pork or lamb, or go for a change with ground chicken. Load up your patties with all the old favorite fixings, or try some fresh new variations such as Napoli Burgers (this page), Provençale Pork Burgers with Peppers (p.68) or Rosemary Lamb Burgers (p.68). Or make a hotdog dinner to satisfy busy, hungry kids. Try an interesting sausage recipe like Beer-Basted Sausage and Pepper on a Roll (p.71). Our ideas will have you making easy fun meals your whole family will love.

NAPOLI BURGERS

Put a little Italian flavor into your barbecuing. Substitute 1/2 tsp (2 mL) each dried basil and oregano if fresh herbs are not available.

1 lb	ground beef	500 g
1	egg	1
1/4 cup	dry bread crumbs	50 mL
1	clove garlic, minced	1
2 tbsp	freshly grated Parmesan cheese	25 mL
1/2 tsp	salt	2 mL
2 tsp	chopped fresh basil	10 mL
1 tsp	chopped fresh oregano	5 mL
1/4 tsp	crushed hot pepper flakes	1 mL
4	slices mozzarella cheese	4
4	Italian rolls or hamburger buns	4
	Garlic butter	
4	slices tomato	4

• In bowl, mix together beef, egg, bread crumbs, garlic, Parmesan cheese, salt, basil, oregano and hot pepper flakes. Divide evenly and shape into 4 patties.
• Cook on greased grill over hot coals or on high setting, turning once, for 10 to 12 minutes or until desired doneness. Top each hamburger with cheese slice; cook just until cheese softens and is slightly melted.
• Meanwhile, split and lightly toast rolls on edge of barbecue; spread with garlic butter. Place hamburger in each bun and top with tomato slice. Makes 4 servings.

(Left to right) Texan Hotdog (sidebar, p. 70); Round Dog with Hot Slaw (p. 70); Napoli Burger

ROSEMARY LAMB BURGERS

Oval patties nestle well in toasted submarine buns. Top with garlicky sauce prepared earlier in the day.

SAUCE:

1 cup	plain yogurt	250 mL
1	clove garlic, minced	1

BURGERS:

1	egg	1
1/4 cup	bread crumbs	50 mL
3 tbsp	plain yogurt	50 mL
1 tbsp	water	15 mL
2	cloves garlic, minced	2
1 tsp	minced fresh rosemary (or 1/4 tsp/1 mL crushed dried)	5 mL
1/2 tsp	salt	2 mL
1/4 tsp	pepper	1 mL
1 lb	ground lamb	500 g

• **Sauce:** Spoon yogurt into fine sieve set over bowl. Let drain for 1 hour in refrigerator. Discard liquid; mix thickened yogurt with garlic. Cover and refrigerate for up to 4 days.
• **Burgers:** In bowl, beat egg; mix in bread crumbs, yogurt, water, garlic, rosemary, salt and pepper. Mix in lamb; shape into 4 oval or flat sausage-shaped patties.
• Cook patties on greased grill over medium-hot coals or on medium-high setting for 5 minutes; turn and cook for about 5 minutes longer or until desired doneness. Makes 4 servings.

PROVENCALE PORK BURGERS WITH PEPPERS

A quick sauté of peppers and onion strips makes a fresh topping for pork patties. Serve in pita pockets.

1	egg	1
1/4 cup	bread crumbs	50 mL
1/4 cup	finely chopped onion	50 mL
2 tbsp	water	25 mL
1	clove garlic, minced	1
1/2 tsp	salt	2 mL
1/2 tsp	dried thyme	2 mL
1/4 tsp	pepper	1 mL
1 lb	lean ground pork	500 g

TOPPING:

1	large onion	1
1	large clove garlic	1
Half	each sweet red and green pepper	Half
1 tbsp	olive oil	15 mL
1/2 tsp	dried oregano	2 mL
Pinch	each salt and pepper	Pinch

• In bowl, beat egg; mix in bread crumbs, onion, water, garlic, salt, thyme and pepper. Mix in pork; shape into 4 patties.
• **Topping:** Cut onion lengthwise into 1/4-inch (5 mm) thick strips. Sliver garlic; cut red and green peppers lengthwise into 1/2-inch (1 cm) thick strips. In small skillet, heat oil over medium heat; cook onion, garlic and red and green peppers, stirring, for about 5 minutes or until softened but not browned. Season with oregano, salt and pepper; keep warm.
• Cook patties on greased grill over medium-hot coals or on medium-high setting for 5 minutes; turn and cook for 10 to 12 minutes longer or until meat is no longer pink inside. Serve with topping. Makes 4 servings.

BETTER BURGERS

Always start with freshly ground meat—preferably packaged the day you're buying—and use it within 1 to 2 days. For beef, a ratio of 80 per cent lean to 20 per cent fat is ideal for juiciness and flavor, making medium ground a good choice. Choose lean ground if you like, but cook it rarer; or choose regular for a very juicy burger, but be prepared for flare-ups on the coals. Look for lean ground pork or lamb. Chicken and turkey are usually lean; you may want to add a touch of butter or oil to these burgers to keep them moist.

When forming patties, handle as little as possible, moulding gently until they're about 3/4 inch (2 cm) thick. Loosely packed (not compact) burgers are crisper on the outside and juicier on the inside.

Put burgers directly on greased grill—or for convenience, use a burger basket over medium-hot coals or on medium-high setting. Cook burgers for 4 to 5 minutes or until browned before turning. Cook for 5 minutes longer for rare, 7 for medium and 10 for well-done burgers.

Instead of plain white hamburger buns, try whole wheat buns or Cheddar, poppy seed, sesame or onion buns. For bagel enthusiasts with a passion for chewing, plain or pumpernickel bagels are great burger holders. Split an English muffin; mould burgers into ovals or sausage shapes and place them in submarine rolls or even croissants. If you love tacos, use big tortillas to encase oval burgers, then add all your favorite taco toppings. All buns are best either split and toasted on the grill, or wrapped in foil and warmed on the barbecue.

Cheddar-Topped Beef Burger

CHEDDAR-TOPPED BEEF BURGERS

An easy Cheddar and mayo topping melts over these burgers on the grill; serve on toasted whole wheat rolls.

3/4 cup	shredded old Cheddar cheese	175 mL
3 tbsp	mayonnaise	50 mL
1/3 cup	chopped green onions	75 mL
2 tbsp	chopped sweet red pepper	25 mL
2 tsp	Dijon mustard	10 mL
1	egg	1
1/4 cup	bread crumbs	50 mL
2 tbsp	water or milk	25 mL
1/2 tsp	salt	2 mL
1/4 tsp	each pepper and dried thyme	1 mL
1 lb	ground beef	500 g

• In small bowl, combine cheese, mayonnaise, 2 tbsp (25 mL) of the onions, red pepper and half of the mustard. Cover and set aside.
• In bowl, beat egg; mix in bread crumbs, water, salt, pepper, thyme, and remaining onions and mustard. Mix in beef; shape into 4 patties.
• Cook patties on greased grill over hot coals or on high setting for 5 minutes; turn and cook for 2 minutes longer. Spread cheese topping over patties and cook for 2 to 3 minutes longer or until desired doneness and cheese has melted. Makes 4 servings.

Hotdogs and sausages on the barbecue

Wieners (hotdogs or franks) are smoked and fully cooked when packaged. All they require is a few quick turns on the grill over hot coals or on high setting to enhance their flavor. Choose pork, beef, chicken or turkey wieners and serve them in every way imaginable—in French bread, pita pockets, rye or pumpernickel bread, onion, sesame or cheese buns and English muffins.

HOTDOG TOPPINGS

Top your hotdogs with good old mustard, relish and ketchup if you want to or try these great alternatives.

Mexican: Guacamole, chopped onion, shredded Cheddar cheese and chopped lettuce.

French: Crumbled chèvre or blue cheese and Dijon mustard.

Italian: Sliced tomatoes and chopped hot or sweet peppers, shredded mozzarella cheese, Parmesan cheese and chopped fresh basil.

Bavarian: Sauerkraut or coleslaw and German-style mustard with poppy seed buns.

Californian: Sliced tomatoes, thin wedges of avocado, alfalfa sprouts on toasted croissants.

Texan: Chili, shredded lettuce and slivered colorful peppers (photo, p. 66).

ROUND DOGS WITH HOT SLAW

Hot slaw surrounded by a wiener circle is an amusing yet tasty treatment for hotdogs. (photo, p.66)

6	wieners	6
6	hamburger buns	6
HOT SLAW:		
1 tsp	vegetable oil	5 mL
1	small onion, thinly sliced	1
2 cups	shredded cabbage	500 mL
1/2 cup	sliced celery	125 mL
1/4 cup	chicken stock or water	50 mL
1 tbsp	soy sauce	15 mL

• Score wieners every 1/2 inch (1 cm), cutting almost through. Using toothpicks, secure ends together, making circle.

• **Hot Slaw:** In large skillet, heat oil over high heat; cook onion, cabbage, celery, stock and soy sauce for 3 to 5 minutes or until vegetables are tender-crisp.

• Cook wieners on greased grill over hot coals or on high setting until blistered and heated through.

• Meanwhile, toast hamburger buns on edge of barbecue. Place wieners in buns; remove toothpicks. Fill centres with hot slaw. Makes 6 servings.

SAUSAGE BAVARIAN STYLE

If you love sausage and sauerkraut, you'll enjoy these hearty hotdogs.

1 lb	bratwurst sausage	500 g
1	bottle (341 mL) beer	1
1	can (14 oz/398 mL) sauerkraut, drained well	1
1/2 cup	sour cream	125 mL
2 tbsp	chopped onion	25 mL
1 tsp	caraway seeds	5 mL
4	large hotdog buns	4
	Hot German mustard	

• Prick skins of sausages and soak in beer for 2 to 3 hours.
• In small saucepan, combine sauerkraut, sour cream, onion and caraway seeds; place on edge of grill just to warm.
• Cook sausages on greased grill over hot coals or on high setting for about 20 minutes or until cooked through. (Alternatively, prick sausages all over; cover with waxed paper and microwave at High for 2 minutes. Turn, prick and cover with waxed paper; microwave at High for 2 to 4 minutes longer or until cooked through. Brown on grill over hot coals or on high setting, turning several times.)
• Meanwhile, toast buns and spread lightly with mustard.
• Slice sausages partway through lengthwise; place in buns and spoon in sauerkraut topping. Makes 4 servings.

BEER-BASTED SAUSAGE AND PEPPER ON A ROLL

Before you brown these sausages over the coals, you can start cooking them either by microwaving or by the conventional method of simmering them in water. A mustardy beer marinade and basting sauce makes good sausages even better. Serve in long crusty rolls.

1 lb	farmer's sausage	500 g
1/2 cup	beef stock	125 mL
1/2 cup	beer	125 mL
1 tbsp	packed brown sugar	15 mL
2 tsp	dry mustard	10 mL
1	clove garlic, minced	1
1	sweet red or green pepper	1
4	long crusty rolls	4

• Place sausages on microwave rack; prick, cover with waxed paper and microwave at High for 2 minutes. Turn, prick and cover with waxed paper; microwave at High for 2 to 4 minutes longer or until cooked through. Let stand for 3 minutes. (Alternatively, in skillet, simmer sausages in water until cooked through, about 12 minutes.) Cut into 1-inch (2.5 cm) lengths.
• In shallow dish, combine beef stock, beer, sugar, mustard and garlic. Add sausage pieces, coating well; cover and marinate in refrigerator for 8 hours, turning often.
• Meanwhile, core and seed red pepper; cut into 1-inch (2.5 cm) squares. Alternately thread sausage and red pepper loosely onto greased metal or soaked wooden skewers.
• Pour marinade into small saucepan; boil, uncovered, for 2 to 3 minutes or until reduced by about one-third.
• Cook kabobs on greased grill over medium-hot coals or on medium-high setting, brushing with beer marinade and turning occasionally, for about 10 minutes or until heated through and browned. Meanwhile, toast halved rolls on grill. Divide sausage and pepper pieces among rolls. Makes 4 servings.

BARBECUING SAUSAGES

Fat, spicy, juicy sausages are delicious smoky and hot from the grill. Fresh pork sausages such as farmer's sausage, knackwurst, bratwurst and sweet and hot Italian sausages are best partially precooked before barbecuing. Bring them to a boil and simmer for 4 to 5 minutes; drain. Alternatively, microwave pricked sausages, covered, at High, for 3 to 4 minutes, or until no longer pink inside, turning once during cooking. Then grill slowly on a greased grill over medium-hot coals or on medium-high setting, turning frequently, for about 10 minutes or until cooked through.

Fully cooked sausages such as wieners, Polish sausage, bologna and smoked sausage need only to be heated over the coals to enhance their flavor.

When buying sausages, check if they're ready-to-serve (cooked) or fresh, and be sure to follow reheating or cooking instructions.

Poultry

Versatile chicken and turkey are just right for light summertime meals and barbecued poultry is succulent and inexpensive. Chicken's mild, delicate flavor suits nearly any seasoning or sauce and turkey is delicious cooked slowly over a spit or over a drip pan in a covered barbecue. Try the unusual Peanutty Chicken Thighs (p.80) and Hoisin-Ginger Chicken Wings (p.77). The Glazed Cornish Hens (p.78) are perfect for a special dinner.

LEMON-ROSEMARY GRILLED CHICKEN

Tender chicken soaked in a lemon-herb marinade, then grilled to golden crispness will become an all-time favorite.

1/3 cup	lemon juice	75 mL
1/4 cup	olive oil	50 mL
2 tbsp	chopped fresh rosemary (or 1 tsp/ 5 mL dried)	25 mL
1	large clove garlic, minced	1
1	chicken (2-1/2 lb/ 1.25 kg)	1
2 tbsp	liquid honey	25 mL
2 tbsp	Dijon mustard	25 mL
	Salt and pepper	

• In small bowl, combine lemon juice, oil, rosemary and garlic. Transfer to shallow glass dish large enough to hold chicken in single layer; set aside.

• Using sharp knife, remove wing tips from chicken. Place bird, breast side down, on cutting board. Using poultry shears or sharp knife, cut along one side of backbone, then along other side; remove and discard backbone. Spread chicken apart to lie flat. Using poultry shears or knife, cut along each side of breastbone to separate into halves. Remove and discard breastbone. Trim off all fat and excess skin.

• Place chicken halves between 2 sheets of plastic wrap. Using smooth mallet, flatten halves for more even cooking.

• Place halves in shallow dish with marinade, turning to coat. Cover and marinate at room temperature for 30 minutes or in refrigerator for 2 hours, turning occasionally. (If marinated in refrigerator, let stand at room temperature for 30 minutes before grilling.)

• Remove halves from marinade; drain well, reserving marinade. Place chicken, bone side down, on grill over medium-hot coals or on medium setting; cook, covered, for 10 to 15 minutes or until golden brown, watching carefully to avoid flare-ups.

• Turn halves over; cook for 10 to 15 minutes or until golden brown. Stir honey and mustard into reserved marinade; brush over chicken and cook, turning and brushing with marinade, for 10 to 15 minutes longer or until juices run clear when chicken is pierced. Season with salt and pepper to taste. Cut halves into quarters to serve. Makes 4 servings.

VARIATIONS:

PEPPERY GRILLED CHICKEN:
• Increase lemon juice to 1/2 cup (125 mL). Substitute 1 tbsp (15 mL) crushed black peppercorns for rosemary. Increase garlic to 2 large cloves.

LIME-CORIANDER GRILLED CHICKEN:
• Substitute lime juice for lemon juice, and add 1 tsp (5 mL) grated lime rind. Substitute vegetable oil for olive oil. Substitute 1 tbsp (15 mL) crushed coriander seeds for rosemary.

Lemon-Rosemary Grilled Chicken

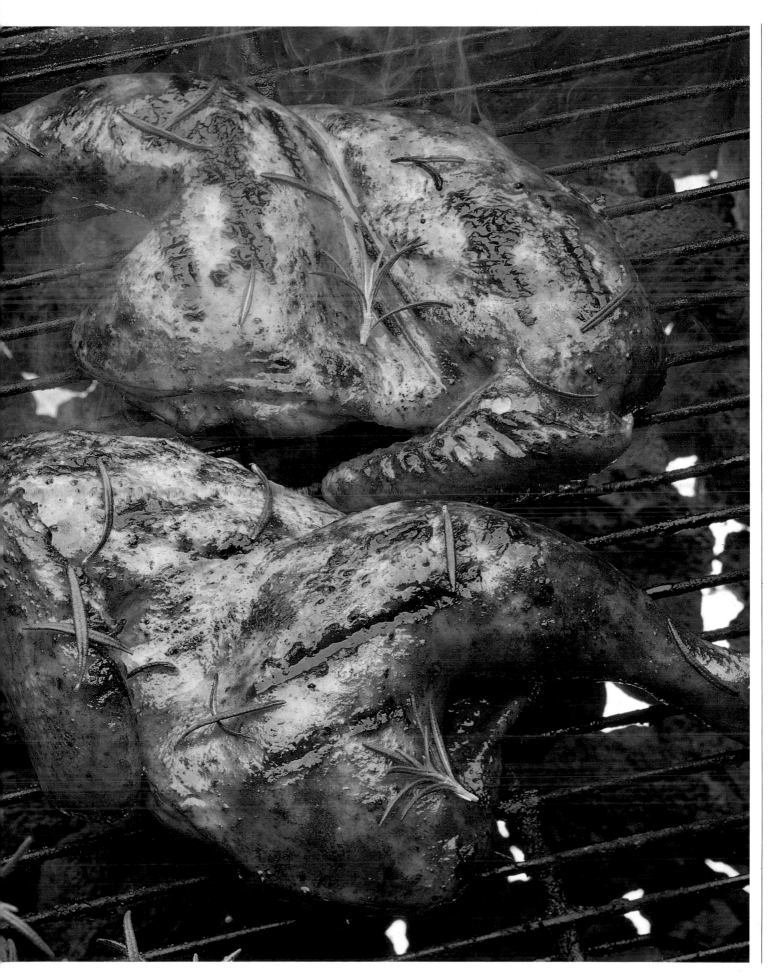

For an interesting mixed grill, you can use half chicken and half boneless veal cutlets, if you prefer.

8	boneless chicken breasts (about 2 lb/ 1 kg total)	8
1/4 cup	minced fresh coriander or parsley	50 mL
1/4 cup	finely chopped shallots*	50 mL
	Salt and pepper	
16	slices pancetta or lean side bacon	16
2 tbsp	cornstarch	25 mL
2 tbsp	dry sherry	25 mL
	Cucumber-Yogurt Sauce, optional (recipe follows)	

MARINADE:

1	onion, minced	1
3/4 cup	lemon juice	175 mL
	Grated rind of 1 lemon	
3 tbsp	light soy sauce	50 mL
2 tbsp	white wine vinegar	25 mL
2 tbsp	liquid honey	25 mL
1 tbsp	minced gingerroot	15 mL
1 tbsp	Dijon mustard	15 mL
2	cloves garlic, minced	2
	Salt and pepper	

CUCUMBER-YOGURT SAUCE:

2	cucumbers, peeled, seeded and diced	2
2 tsp	salt	10 mL
1-1/2 cups	plain yogurt	375 mL
1 cup	sour cream	250 mL
2	cloves garlic, minced	2
1 tsp	lemon juice	5 mL
1 tbsp	chopped fresh dill (or 1 tsp/5 mL dried dillweed)	15 mL
	Salt and pepper	

• **Marinade:** In shallow glass or ceramic dish just large enough to hold chicken in single layer, combine onion, lemon juice, rind, soy sauce, vinegar, honey, ginger, mustard, garlic and salt and pepper to taste. Add chicken and spoon marinade over. Cover and marinate at room temperature for at least 2 hours or refrigerate overnight.

• Drain chicken, reserving marinade. Pat chicken dry and place between 2 sheets of waxed paper; pound with mallet until flattened.

• Combine coriander, shallots, and salt and pepper to taste; spoon about 2 tsp (10 mL) onto each chicken breast and roll up. Wrap 2 slices pancetta around each breast and secure with small skewers, if necessary.

• Pour marinade into saucepan and bring to boil. Combine cornstarch with sherry; stir into marinade. Set pan on edge of grill.

• Cook chicken on greased grill over medium-hot coals or on medium setting, brushing once or twice with marinade, for 7 to 8 minutes on each side or until chicken is no longer pink inside. Serve with Cucumber-Yogurt Sauce (if using). Makes 6 to 8 servings.

*If shallots are unavailable, you can substitute 1 small onion, finely chopped, and 1 clove garlic, minced.

• In colander, sprinkle cucumbers with salt; let drain for 30 minutes. Rinse and pat dry with paper towels.

• Transfer cucumbers to serving bowl; stir in yogurt, sour cream, garlic, lemon juice, dill, and salt and pepper to taste. Cover and refrigerate for at least 1 hour before serving. Makes about 3 cups (750 mL).

To ensure that chicken will be crisp and browned on the outside and cooked through evenly, cook over medium heat. Flatten chicken and begin grilling bone side down; the bones diffuse the heat evenly through the meat. To prevent scorching, use sugar-based or tomato sauces during the last 10 to 15 minutes of cooking time only.

(Clockwise from top) Cauliflower and Red Pepper Salad (p. 109); Vegetable Kabobs (p. 122); sliced tomatoes; Grilled Chicken Breasts with Pancetta

SPICY GRILLED CHICKEN

A piquant marinade adds flavor to the chicken and prevents it from drying out during grilling.

4 lb	chicken pieces	2 kg
MARINADE:		
1/3 cup	vegetable oil	75 mL
2 tbsp	lime juice	25 mL
2	cloves garlic, crushed	2
1-1/2 tsp	finely chopped fresh oregano (or 1/2 tsp/2 mL dried)	7 mL
1 tsp	salt	5 mL
1/2 tsp	grated lime rind	2 mL
1/4 tsp	crushed dried chilies	1 mL
1/4 tsp	pepper	1 mL

• **Marinade:** In shallow glass or ceramic dish, stir together oil, lime juice, garlic, oregano, salt, lime rind, chilies and pepper. Add chicken and let stand at room temperature for 1 hour, turning occasionally. Drain chicken, reserving marinade.

• Arrange chicken, skin side up, on lightly greased grill over medium-hot coals or on medium setting; cook, turning often and basting with marinade, for about 30 to 40 minutes or until chicken is no longer pink near bone. Makes 6 to 8 servings.

Mop Sauce Chicken

MOP SAUCE CHICKEN

"Mop" chicken legs with our chili sauce and serve with a cabbage-carrot slaw and foil-wrapped potatoes baked over the coals.

4	chicken legs (about 2 lb/1 kg total)	4
2 tbsp	vegetable oil	25 mL
1/2 tsp	black pepper	2 mL
Pinch	cayenne pepper	Pinch
	Salt	

MOP SAUCE:		
2 tbsp	butter	25 mL
1	onion, minced	1
1	large clove garlic, minced	1
1 cup	chili sauce, puréed	250 mL
1 cup	water	250 mL
2 tbsp	cider vinegar	25 mL
1 tbsp	horseradish	15 mL
1 tbsp	Worcestershire sauce	15 mL
1 tsp	dry mustard	5 mL
1/2 tsp	each dried marjoram and thyme	2 mL
Pinch	pepper	Pinch
	Salt	

• **Mop Sauce:** In heavy saucepan, melt butter over medium heat; cook onion and garlic until softened, 3 to 5 minutes. Stir in chili sauce, water, vinegar, horseradish, Worcestershire sauce, mustard, marjoram, thyme and pepper. Bring to boil, stirring constantly. Reduce heat; simmer, uncovered and stirring occasionally, until thickened, about 20 minutes. Season with salt to taste.

• Meanwhile, trim any fat from chicken. Brush chicken lightly with oil. Sprinkle with black and cayenne peppers. Cook chicken on greased grill over medium-hot coals or on medium setting, for 30 to 40 minutes or until chicken is crusty brown but no longer pink inside, turning often and "mopping" with sauce during last 10 minutes. Season with salt to taste. Makes 4 servings.

HOISIN-GINGER CHICKEN WINGS

This teriyaki-type sauce with the extra flavor of hoisin sauce makes a scrumptious marinade for chicken wings.

3 lb	chicken wings	1.5 kg
MARINADE:		
1/3 cup	soy sauce	75 mL
1/4 cup	hoisin sauce*	50 mL
1/4 cup	rice vinegar	50 mL
3 tbsp	packed brown sugar	50 mL
4	cloves garlic, minced	4
1 tbsp	vegetable oil	15 mL
2 tsp	minced gingerroot	10 mL
1 tsp	sesame oil	5 mL
1/4 tsp	crushed dried hot pepper flakes	1 mL

- **Marinade:** In bowl, combine soy sauce, hoisin sauce, vinegar, sugar, garlic, vegetable oil, gingerroot, sesame oil and hot pepper flakes; mix well.
- Place chicken in plastic bag and pour in marinade; seal bag and place in large bowl. Refrigerate for at least 3 hours or for up to 48 hours, turning bag occasionally.
- Cook wings on greased grill over hot coals or on high setting, turning to prevent burning, for 25 to 30 minutes or until chicken is no longer pink inside. Makes about 6 main-course servings.

*Available at some supermarkets and most Chinese food stores.

HERB AND GARLIC CHICKEN LEGS

A seasoned butter stuffed under the skin helps to flavor and moisten grilled chicken. Remember to keep a spray bottle filled with water nearby to douse any flare-ups.

4	chicken legs (2 lb/1 kg total)	4
1/4 cup	butter	50 mL
2 tbsp	finely chopped fresh parsley	25 mL
2 tbsp	finely chopped green onion	25 mL
1	clove garlic, minced	1
	Pepper	
	Vegetable oil	

- Gently loosen skin on thigh end of each chicken leg to make large pocket.
- Cream together butter, parsley, onion, garlic, and pepper to taste. Divide into 4 portions and insert into pockets under skin of chicken legs, pressing down gently to spread herb butter over thigh; brush chicken legs with oil.
- Cook chicken, skin side up, on lightly greased grill over medium-hot coals or on medium setting for 20 minutes. Turn chicken over; cook for 10 to 20 minutes longer or until juices run clear when chicken is pierced with skewer and meat is no longer pink near bone. Makes 4 servings.

BARBECUED LEMON CHICKEN

Here's an easy delectable chicken dish.

1/4 cup	lemon juice	50 mL
1/4 cup	vegetable oil	50 mL
1/2 tsp	dried thyme (or 2 tsp/10 mL chopped fresh)	2 mL
1 tsp	black peppercorns	5 mL
2-1/2 lb	chicken, halved or cut in pieces	1.25 kg

- Combine lemon juice, oil and thyme. Coarsely grind or crush pepper; add to lemon mixture. Place chicken in shallow dish; pour lemon mixture over, turning chicken to coat all over. Refrigerate for 1 to 3 hours, turning chicken occasionally.
- Cook chicken on greased grill over medium-hot coals or on medium setting, turning frequently to prevent burning, for about 30 to 45 minutes or until chicken is no longer pink inside. Makes about 4 servings.

BARBECUING TURKEY AND CHICKEN PARTS

ON THE GRILL

Turkey parts: Wrap the turkey parts in heavy foil, dull side out, and place on the grill 6 to 8 inches (15 to 20 cm) from the heat source. Barbecue for 1 hour, turning occasionally. (Wings can be added 30 minutes after other parts.) Remove all the turkey parts from the foil, place directly on grill and brush with marinade. Continue cooking, turning the parts often until meat is fork-tender, about 30 to 40 minutes.

Chicken parts: Place the chicken directly on the grill; brush with vegetable oil or marinade and turn frequently to prevent burning. Barbecue for 7 to 8 minutes per side for wings, 6 to 7 minutes per side for boneless breasts, 30 to 40 minutes for pieces and 50 to 55 minutes for chicken halves.

IN A BASKET ON THE SPIT

Place marinated turkey or chicken parts in wire basket (available in hardware stores) and place on spit. Barbecue 1 to 1-1/2 hours or until meat is tender.

CHICKEN BROCHETTES

Flavored with pimientos and shallots and spiked with a hint of hot pepper, these marinated brochettes are delicious, either as an appetizer or served on rice along with a green salad for a main course.

1/2 cup	vegetable oil	125 mL
1	jar (4-1/2 oz/128 mL) pimientos, drained	1
2 tbsp	red wine vinegar	25 mL
2	large shallots, minced	2
1	large clove garlic, minced	1
1 tsp	salt	5 mL
1/4 tsp	crushed hot pepper flakes	1 mL
1/2 tsp	ground cumin	2 mL
	Pepper	
1-1/2 lb	boneless skinless chicken breasts (about 6)	750 g

• In blender or food processor, combine oil, pimientos, vinegar, shallots, garlic, salt, hot pepper flakes, cumin, and pepper to taste; process for about 20 seconds or until blended.
• Cut chicken into 1/2-inch (1 cm) cubes for appetizers, or 1-inch (2.5 cm) cubes for main course. Place chicken in shallow dish and pour pimiento mixture over; stir to coat all pieces. Cover and refrigerate for up to 2 days, stirring occasionally.
• Thread chicken onto greased metal or soaked wooden skewers. For appetizers, break wooden skewers in half or use toothpicks. Cook on greased grill over hot coals or on high setting, turning to prevent burning, for 10 to 20 minutes, depending on size of chicken cubes, or until chicken is no longer pink inside. Makes about 6 main-course servings.

GLAZED CORNISH HENS

As well as keeping the birds moist, fresh plums add a touch of color and an intriguing flavor to the delicate taste of Cornish hens. If plums are not available, substitute 1 can (14 oz/398 mL) prune plums, drained, pitted and blended with 1/2 cup (125 mL) reserved juice instead of the orange juice.

2	large blue or red plums or 6 small prune plums	2
1/2 cup	orange juice	125 mL
2 tbsp	packed brown sugar	25 mL
2 tbsp	chili sauce	25 mL
1 tsp	lemon juice	5 mL
1/2 tsp	salt	2 mL
1/4 tsp	hot pepper sauce	1 mL
4	Cornish hens (about 1 lb/500 g each)	4
	Salt and pepper	
GARNISH:		
	Plum halves and fresh parsley	

• Pit plums and place in blender or food processor along with orange juice, sugar, chili sauce, lemon juice, salt and hot pepper sauce. Blend until smooth. Transfer to saucepan; heat to boiling. (Alternatively, microwave at High for 2-1/2 to 3 minutes, stirring twice.) Remove from heat; set aside.
• Wash hens and dry with paper towels. Sprinkle cavities lightly with salt and pepper to taste. Tie legs together and tie wings tightly to body.
• Place hens on greased grill over drip pan; cover and cook over medium-hot coals or on medium setting for 20 minutes. Brush with plum mixture; cook, brushing several times with plum mixture, for 20 to 30 minutes longer or until meat is no longer pink near bone.
• **Garnish:** Arrange hens on platter and garnish with plum halves and parsley. Heat any remaining sauce and spoon over top. Makes 4 servings.

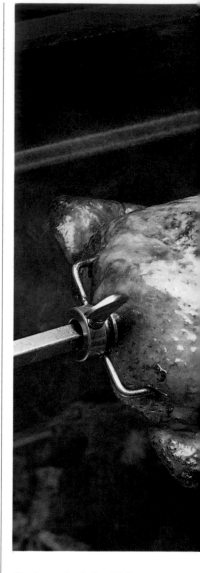

Barbecued whole chickens

BARBECUING WHOLE BIRDS

Follow this guide for perfectly cooked chicken and turkey. Cook enough to have leftovers for turkey or chicken salad.

ON THE ROTISSERIE

Turkeys under 12 lb (6 kg) and broiler/ fryer chickens are best for the barbecue rotisserie. Rinse the bird under cold water and pat dry. Season the cavity with herbs or sprinkle with salt and lemon juice.

Tie the wings securely to the body and the legs to the tail. (Picture wire or kitchen twine works well.) Then insert the spit in front of the tail and through the bird so that it is balanced on the spit. Fasten the bird securely with the spit forks at both ends. Four-pronged spit forks work best to hold the heavier weight of turkeys.

For tastier crisp skin, brush the bird

with a mixture of one part vegetable oil, one part butter and one part lemon juice.

To prevent flare-ups, use a drip pan (such as a disposable baking pan or make one out of heavy-duty foil) containing water or sand. On a gas barbecue, use a low to medium flame for chicken and a low flame for turkey. With a charcoal barbecue add more coals after one hour.

To test for doneness, turn off the rotisserie motor and insert a meat thermometer into the thickest part of the thigh. Close the lid and after 5 minutes, check the reading. The bird is cooked when it reaches a temperature of 180° to 185°F (83° to 85°C).

ON THE GRILL

Barbecuing a bird on the grill works best if your barbecue has a cover. With a gas barbecue, place the whole bird on a rack in a shallow pan on the grill. Or

place the bird directly on the grill with a drip pan underneath. With a charcoal barbecue, arrange the coals near the outer edges with the drip pan on the floor of the barbecue under the bird.

BARBECUING TIMES FOR WHOLE BIRDS	
Turkeys	
Weight	**Approximate Time***
6 lb (3 kg)	3 hours
8 lb (3.5 kg)	3-1/2 hours
10 lb (4.5 kg)	4 hours
12 lb (5.5 kg)	4-1/2 hours
Chickens	
3 lb (1.5 kg)	1 to 1-1/2 hours
4 to 5 lb (2 kg)	1-1/2 to 2 hours

*Times may be slightly longer if uncovered, on a rotisserie. Poultry is cooked when meat thermometer reads 180° to 185°F (83° to 85°C).

PEANUTTY CHICKEN THIGHS

If you love peanut butter, you'll love the flavor it adds to barbecued chicken. Garnish this dish with fresh coriander and serve with rice and a yogurt-dressed cucumber and radish salad.

8	chicken thighs (about 2-1/2 lb/ 1.25 kg total)	8
2 tbsp	vegetable oil	25 mL
1/2 tsp	pepper	2 mL
	Salt	
PEANUTTY SAUCE:		
1/4 cup	vegetable oil	50 mL
1	onion, minced	1
2	cloves garlic, minced	2
1/4 tsp	hot pepper flakes	1 mL
1/4 cup	water	50 mL
1/4 cup	smooth peanut butter	50 mL
2 tbsp	light soy sauce	25 mL
2 tbsp	lemon juice	25 mL
2 tbsp	minced fresh coriander (optional)	25 mL
1/4 tsp	salt	1 mL

• **Peanutty Sauce:** In small skillet, heat oil over medium heat; cook onion, garlic and hot pepper flakes until softened, about 5 minutes. In bowl, combine onion mixture with water, peanut butter, soy sauce, lemon juice, coriander (if using) and salt. Set aside.

• Brush chicken with oil; sprinkle with pepper. Cook on greased grill over medium-hot coals or on medium setting for 30 to 40 minutes or until chicken is crusty brown but no longer pink inside, turning often and brushing with Peanutty Sauce during last 10 minutes of cooking. Season with salt to taste. Makes 4 servings.

TANDOORI CHICKEN

Serve this light Indian-style chicken with rice pilaf and accompany with raita *(cucumber and yogurt salad) or an avocado and tomato salad.*

1 tbsp	Dijon mustard	15 mL
1/2 cup	vegetable oil	125 mL
1/2 cup	plain yogurt	125 mL
1 tbsp	minced gingerroot	15 mL
1/2 tsp	each cumin and coriander seeds	2 mL
1/2 tsp	ground turmeric	2 mL
	Juice of 1 lemon	
1	can (4 oz/110 g) green chili peppers (or 1 fresh green chili pepper), seeded and chopped	1
5 lb	chicken pieces (or 2 chickens cut in pieces)	2.5 kg
1	head Boston lettuce (optional)	1

• Place mustard in mixing bowl or food processor; very gradually add oil, whisking or processing, as if making mayonnaise, until well blended. Stir in yogurt and set aside.

• Using mortar and pestle or mini-chopper, pound or grind together gingerroot, cumin, coriander and turmeric to form paste. Add lemon juice and mix until well combined; stir into yogurt mixture along with green chili peppers.

• Remove skin from chicken. Using sharp knife, make small shallow cuts about 1 inch (2.5 cm) apart in meat. Place in shallow dish or plastic bag and pour yogurt mixture over; stir to coat all pieces. Cover and refrigerate for at least 8 hours or for up to 24 hours.

• Cook chicken on greased grill over medium-hot coals or on medium setting, turning as necessary to prevent burning, for 15 to 20 minutes on each side or until chicken is no longer pink inside.

• Line serving platter with lettuce leaves (if using); arrange chicken on top. Makes 8 to 10 servings.

WINTER BARBECUING

Barbecuing is no longer just a summer activity.

• *If you grill outside during the winter, cooking times will vary from our recipes which have been tested indoors.*

• *Test vegetables or quick-cooking foods, like lamb or shrimp, by touch and appearance as indicated in the recipes.*

• *A meat thermometer is invaluable for checking large cuts of meat.*

• *Make sure the coals or rocks are hot enough before starting to cook. If using charcoal, you won't be able to hold your hand over a medium-hot fire for more than three or four seconds, and the coals will be covered with grey ash through which a red glow is just visible.*

• *If using a gas barbecue, allow the usual 10 to 15 minutes of preheating.*

• *If you don't have a barbecue cover, you can reduce the effect of cooling winter winds by making one. Clip off and discard the hooks of six wire coat hangers. Straighten hangers and twist together the ends of two or three to make a circle that fits over your grill. Bend the rest to form half circles and attach to the circle like umbrella ribs. Cover the frame with heavy-duty foil.*

Smoked Turkey

SMOKED TURKEY

Smoked poultry retains a pink color when cooked: use a meat thermometer to ensure doneness (See Smoke Cooking, p. 52).

1	turkey (12 to 15 lb/ 6 to 7 kg)	1
3	onions, quartered	3
2	stalks celery, cut in chunks	2
1	lemon, sliced	1
CURE:		
1 cup	pickling salt	250 mL
1/4 cup	packed brown sugar	50 mL
1 tsp	each dried sage and thyme	5 mL
LIQUID FOR WATER PAN:		
1/2 cup	butter	125 mL
3	cloves garlic, crushed	3
1/4 cup	lemon juice	50 mL
2 cups	white wine or chicken stock	500 mL

• Rinse turkey with cold water and pat dry.
• **Cure:** In small bowl, combine salt, sugar, sage and thyme; rub over turkey and into cavities. Wrap turkey in large plastic bag (not foil); refrigerate for 6 to 8 hours or overnight. Rinse turkey under cold running water; dry well. Place onions, celery and lemon inside cavity.
• **Liquid for Water Pan:** In saucepan, melt butter; stir in garlic and lemon juice. Soak double thickness of cheesecloth in some of the butter mixture and drape over turkey.
• Add wine to remaining butter mixture; heat just to boiling. Pour into water pan set over hot coals and soaked wood chips.
• Place turkey on rack above water pan; cover smoker and smoke-cook for about 8 hours or until leg joint moves easily and meat thermometer in thigh registers 180°F (85°C). Remove cheesecloth for last hour of cooking. Makes about 15 servings.

Fish and Seafood

Fish and seafood are perfect summertime foods, quick to cook, calorie-light and delectable. Because fish cooks so quickly, it barbecues to perfection in minutes and the taste is out of this world. Nearly all common freshwater and saltwater fish, fresh or frozen (defrosted of course), can be cooked on a barbecue. The most important rule to remember for fish is not to overcook it! Be sure to follow our tips and tests for doneness. Here you'll find delicious smoked fish recipes like Fennel-Smoked Trout with Lemon Butter (p.84) and Hickory-Smoked Fish (p.87) to seafood delicacies like Shrimp and Scallop Kabobs (p.87) and easy dishes like Fish with Ginger Sauce (p.88).

GRILL-POACHED STUFFED PIKE

"Grill-poaching" in foil is an easy way to barbecue large whole fish, such as salmon, lake trout, pike and bass. The stuffing adds savory goodness.

1	whole pike, cleaned, head and tail intact (about 2.5 lb/1.25 kg)	1
	Butter	
1	lemon, sliced	1
STUFFING:		
1 cup	crushed croutons or coarse dry bread crumbs	250 mL
1/2 cup	chopped watercress	125 mL
1 tbsp	unsalted butter	15 mL
1/2 cup	chopped mushrooms	125 mL
2 tbsp	chopped shallots	25 mL
2 tbsp	lemon juice	25 mL
Pinch	each salt and pepper	Pinch
GARNISH:		
	Watercress sprigs	
	Cherry tomatoes	
	Lemon wedges	

Grill-Poached Stuffed Pike; Shrimp and Scallop Kabobs (p. 87); Fennel-Smoked Trout with Lemon Butter (p. 84)

- **Stuffing:** In bowl, mix together croutons and watercress. In small skillet, melt butter over low heat; cook mushrooms and shallots, covered, for about 5 minutes or until softened. Stir into crouton mixture along with lemon juice, salt and pepper; mix well.
- Rinse fish inside and out; pat dry. Fill cavity with stuffing; skewer or sew fish closed (or secure with string).
- Butter shiny side of piece of heavy-duty foil large enough to enclose fish. Place half of the lemon slices on foil and place fish on top. Top fish with remaining lemon slices. Draw edges of foil up over fish to form loose package, double-folding edges and crimping to seal tightly.
- Cook package on well-greased covered grill over medium-hot coals or on medium setting, turning occasionally, for 20 to 25 minutes or until flesh is opaque and flakes easily when tested with fork.
- **Garnish:** To serve, unwrap fish and place on large warmed platter. Debone and cut into thick individual pieces. Garnish with watercress, tomatoes and lemon wedges. Makes 4 servings.

FENNEL-SMOKED TROUT WITH LEMON BUTTER

Besides flavored chips and coals, herbal branches or leaves laid directly on the coals can enhance barbecued foods. Lemon balm, bay or fennel complement fish. Soak the herb in water to prevent scorching during grilling, then cook fish in the herb-scented smoke. Mild-flavored, firm-fleshed fish, such as trout and turbot, are best for this treatment. (photo, p.82)

1	fennel bulb	1
1-1/2 lb	trout or turbot fillets	750 g
1 tbsp	vegetable oil	15 mL
1	small lemon, cut in half	1
1/2 cup	unsalted butter	125 mL

• Cutting down to bulb, cut off 3 or 4 fennel stalks and soak in bowl of cold water for about 1 hour. Chop fennel leaves to make 1 tbsp (15 mL) and set aside. (Reserve bulb for another use, such as side dish cooked in cream sauce.)
• Rinse fillets and pat dry. Brush with oil and sprinkle with juice of half the lemon; place in greased hinged wire grill. Drain fennel stalks and place directly on medium-hot coals or rocks. Cover barbecue and cook fillets for about 3 minutes on each side or until flesh is opaque and flakes easily with fork.
• Meanwhile, in small saucepan, melt butter; add juice from remaining lemon half. Blend in reserved 1 tbsp (15 mL) chopped fennel leaves. Spoon over fillets and serve immediately. Pass any remaining butter separately. Makes 4 servings.

SMOKED WHOLE TROUT

If your smoker has more than one rack, prepare extra trout and freeze after smoking (See Smoke Cooking, p. 52).

1	rainbow trout (about 6 lb/3 kg)	1
	Vegetable oil	
1	lemon, sliced	1
	Chopped fresh dill	
CURE:		
1 cup	pickling salt	250 mL
1/4 cup	packed brown sugar	50 mL
1 tsp	celery seeds	5 mL
	Pepper	
LIQUID FOR WATER PAN:		
3 cups	chicken stock	750 mL
1 cup	white wine	250 mL
1	lemon, sliced	1
SAUCE:		
1 cup	sour cream	250 mL
2 tbsp	Dijon mustard	25 mL
1 tbsp	lemon juice	15 mL
	Pepper	

• **Cure:** In small bowl, combine salt, sugar, celery seeds, and pepper to taste. Rub over fish; place on platter and let stand at room temperature for 3 hours. Rinse fish under cold running water; dry well.
• Brush fish inside and out with oil; place lemon slices and handful of dill inside cavity. Set aside.
• **Liquid for Water Pan:** In saucepan, combine stock and wine; bring to boil. Pour into water pan set over hot coals and soaked wood chips; add lemon slices.
• Place fish on rack above water pan (cut fish in half crosswise if necessary). Cover smoker and smoke-cook for about 5 hours or until fish flakes easily when tested with fork.
• **Sauce:** Meanwhile, in small bowl, combine sour cream, mustard, lemon juice, and pepper to taste. Cover and refrigerate until serving time. Pass sauce separately. Makes 12 very generous servings.

SMOKE COOKING WITHOUT THE SMOKER

Get the rich color, a light woodsy taste and the juiciness of smoke cooking even if you don't have a smoker. You can add a smoke flavor in any barbecue with a tight-fitting hood by adding dampened wood chips to the coals.
• *Use chips or chunks of hardwoods or fruitwoods such as mesquite, hickory, oak, alder, walnut, maple, cherry, peach or grapevine clippings (that have not been sprayed with chemicals). Don't use softwoods like pine or spruce which give off an unpleasant flavor.*
• *Soak wood chips for at least 30 minutes and chunks for one to two hours. Scatter a few damp chips directly onto the hot coals or set in foil pan set inside another foil pan containing water, on the lava rocks or flavor bars.*
• *Other flavoring agents impart good flavors to barbecued foods, too. Nuts work well; crack with a hammer before soaking. Dried seaweed complements fish. Herbs and spices (whole cinnamon sticks, whole nutmeg, garlic cloves) and dried orange or lemon peel can be soaked then sprinkled over coals or lava rocks for added flavor.*

Trout in Lettuce Leaves;
Potatoes Deluxe (p. 124);
Baked Pineapple (p. 27)

TROUT IN LETTUCE LEAVES

Fresh trout is nicest, but frozen will do if thawed completely before cooking. The lettuce keeps the fish moist during cooking, so be sure the leaves are as long or longer than the trout. You could also overlap two leaves if necessary.

6	trout, cleaned and heads removed	6
	Salt and pepper	
12	romaine leaves	12
12	thin slices lemon	12
12	thin slices onion	12
1/4 cup	butter	50 mL

• Pat each trout dry with paper towels; sprinkle cavities with salt and pepper.

• Rinse romaine leaves in cold water; shake off excess but do not dry. Place 1 leaf on flat surface. Top with 1 lemon slice and 1 onion slice, separated into rings. Place 1 trout on top, then 1 lemon slice and another onion slice separated into rings. Dot with 2 tsp (10 mL) butter and place another leaf on top.

• Tie whole bundle together with string, wrapping lettuce tightly around fish. Repeat with remaining ingredients. (Fish can be prepared ahead to this point, covered with wet towels and refrigerated for up to 2 hours.)

• Cover and cook on greased grill over medium-hot coals or on medium setting, turning bundles once, for 15 minutes or until fish flakes easily when unwrapped and tested with fork. Remove leaves and serve. Makes 6 servings.

SALMON AND SCALLOP KABOBS WITH LIME-BUTTER SAUCE

Serve with a salad of marinated tiny green beans and tomatoes. Grill slices of parboiled new potatoes along with the kabobs.

1 lb	salmon steaks	500 g
1/2 lb	scallops	250 g
2 tbsp	lime juice	25 mL
1/2 tsp	pepper	2 mL
1/3 cup	unsalted butter	75 mL
2	small cloves garlic, minced	2
2 tbsp	chopped fresh parsley	25 mL
2	limes, quartered	2

• Cut salmon and scallops into even-sized pieces; place in glass bowl. Sprinkle with lime juice and pepper. Let stand at room temperature for 30 minutes.
• With slotted spoon, remove salmon and scallops; set aside. Pour marinade into saucepan and stir in butter and garlic; heat over low heat until butter has melted. Remove from heat; stir in parsley.
• Alternately thread salmon, scallops and 2 lime quarters each onto 4 long greased metal skewers; brush well with lime-butter sauce. Cook kabobs on greased grill over medium-hot coals or on medium-high setting, brushing often with sauce, for 8 to 10 minutes or until scallops are opaque and fish flakes easily when tested with fork. Makes 4 servings.

Salmon and Scallop Kabobs with Lime-Butter Sauce

BARBECUING SHELLFISH

Mussels: Discard any that do not close or have gaping or broken shells. Scrub under cold running water, grasp firmly and pull away the beard. Store in refrigerator in bowl or paper bag. Place mussels on grill over very hot coals or on high setting; cover grill or close

barbecue. Cook for 3 to 5 minutes or until mussels gape open. Discard any that do not open after cooking.

Clams: Select clams that are firmly shut. Scrub under cold running water and store in refrigerator in bowl or paper bag. Cook clams over very hot coals or on high setting for 5 to 7 minutes or until they gape open. Discard any that open only slightly or do not open.

Oysters: Select oysters that are tightly shut. Don't use ones whose shells feel springy when pressed between thumb and forefinger. Scrub under cold running water and store in refrigerator in bowl or paper bag. Cook oysters, flat shell up, over hot coals or on high setting for 4 to 6 minutes or until opened slightly. Discard any that do not open. Wearing oven mitts, hold oyster and insert knife to twist off flat shell. Cut oyster away from flat shell if necessary and place in curved shell.

Lobsters: Have your fishmonger split and butterfly fresh lobster for grilling. If using frozen lobster tails, defrost completely in refrigerator before cooking. Brush cut surfaces of lobster with melted butter. Cook, shell-side down, over hot coals or on high setting for 6 to 7 minutes, turning once, or until meat is opaque and starts to separate from shell. Remember— overcooking toughens lobster.

SHRIMP AND SCALLOP KABOBS

The shrimp and scallops can be marinated overnight and the kabobs assembled several hours before grilling. (photo, p.82)

10 to 12	fresh sea scallops, 1/2 inch (1 cm) thick (1 lb/500 g total)	10 to 12
8	large fresh shrimp (1/2 lb/250 g total)	8
3	lemons	3
1	large sweet red pepper	1
8	mushrooms	8
	Chopped green onions (optional)	
MARINADE:		
1/4 cup	vegetable oil	50 mL
1/4 cup	dry white wine or lemon juice	50 mL
1/2 tsp	grated gingerroot	2 mL
1	small clove garlic, minced	1
2 tbsp	chopped fresh fennel leaves or dill	25 mL
1	green onion, chopped	1

• **Marinade:** In small bowl, blend together oil, wine, gingerroot, garlic, fennel and onion; divide between 2 bowls.

• Rinse scallops and pat dry; place in one bowl of marinade, tossing to coat. Peel and devein shrimp, leaving tail shells intact; place in second bowl of marinade, tossing to coat. Cover bowls and refrigerate for 2 to 3 hours, stirring several times. Remove seafood from marinade; strain marinade and reserve.

• Cut each lemon into 4 thick slices. Cut red pepper in half; seed and cut each half into quarters.

• To assemble kabobs, alternately thread scallops, shrimp, lemon slices, red pepper pieces and mushrooms onto 4 greased metal skewers. Brush with some of the reserved marinade.

• Cook kabobs over medium-hot coals or on medium setting for 10 minutes or until shrimp are bright pink, turning often and basting occasionally with marinade. Sprinkle with green onions (if using) and serve immediately. Makes 4 servings.

HICKORY-SMOKED FISH

The smoke from soaked hickory chips sprinkled on the hot coals adds a fabulous smoky flavor to fresh fish. Smoke-cook a double batch, then wrap and refrigerate half of it for a delicious chilled appetizer or salad the following day.

6	fish steaks or fillets (salmon, halibut, whitefish), 3/4 to 1 inch (2 to 2.5 cm) thick	6
2 tbsp	vegetable oil	25 mL
2 tbsp	lemon juice	25 mL
1 tbsp	packed brown sugar	15 mL
1 tsp	dried dillweed	5 mL
1/2 tsp	salt	2 mL

• Place fish in large bowl. Combine oil, lemon juice, sugar, dillweed and salt; stir until sugar dissolves. Pour over fish and refrigerate for 1 hour, turning once.

• Remove fish from marinade, reserving marinade. In lightly greased baking dish or foil pan, arrange fish in single layer; place on heavy-duty foil on grill over low heat or on low setting. Close hood and cook, turning fish once and basting with marinade several times, for 30 to 40 minutes or until fish flakes easily when tested with fork. Makes 6 servings.

FISH WITH GINGER SAUCE

This sauce is good with salmon, monkfish, pickerel, halibut or any other mild-flavored fish firm enough to barbecue. Add wet hickory chips to the coals for an intriguing smoky flavor.

1-1/2 lb	fish fillets or steaks	750 g
	Salt and pepper	
1/2 cup	tomato sauce	125 mL
1/4 cup	chicken stock	50 mL
2 tbsp	soy sauce	25 mL
1 tbsp	vinegar	15 mL
1 tbsp	liquid honey	15 mL
2 tsp	finely chopped gingerroot	10 mL
Dash	hot pepper sauce	Dash

• Sprinkle fish lightly with salt and pepper to taste; set aside.
• Combine tomato sauce, stock, soy sauce, vinegar, honey, gingerroot and hot pepper sauce. Brush over both sides of fish.
• Cook fish on well-greased grill over medium-hot coals or on medium setting for 8 minutes. Turn and cook for 5 minutes longer, depending on thickness of fish, or until fish flakes easily when tested with fork. Bring remaining marinade to boil and serve as sauce. Makes 6 servings.

GRILLED FISH FILLETS WITH LEMON-BASIL BUTTER

This flavorful marinade and basting sauce complements halibut, mackerel, cod and carp fillets. For easy turning and nonstick grilling, use a greased hinged wire fish grill.

1-1/2 lb	fish fillets	750 g
MARINADE:		
1/2 cup	vegetable oil	125 mL
1 tbsp	dry white wine, vermouth or lemon juice	15 mL
1 tbsp	chopped fresh parsley	15 mL
1 tbsp	chopped fresh oregano (or 1 tsp/ 5 mL dried)	15 mL
1 tsp	Dijon mustard	5 mL
1	small clove garlic, minced	1
Pinch	pepper	Pinch
LEMON-BASIL BUTTER:		
1/2 cup	unsalted butter, softened	125 mL
2 tbsp	lemon juice	25 mL
4	fresh basil leaves	4

• **Lemon-Basil Butter:** In small bowl, blend butter with lemon juice. Cut basil leaves by folding in half and slicing into thin strips; stir into butter mixture. Cover and refrigerate for several hours or overnight.
• **Marinade:** In shallow dish, blend together oil, wine, parsley, oregano, mustard, garlic and pepper. Rinse fillets and pat dry. Place in marinade, turning to coat both sides. Marinate for 1 to 2 hours in refrigerator, turning occasionally.
• Drain fillets, reserving marinade; cook in greased hinged wire fish grill over medium-hot coals or on medium setting, basting occasionally with marinade, for 4 minutes on each side or until fish is opaque and flakes easily when tested with fork. Serve immediately and top with some of the flavored butter. Pass any remaining butter separately. Makes 4 servings.

Fish with Ginger Sauce

GRILLED MONKFISH WITH CUMIN AND LIME

Grilled Monkfish with Cumin and Lime

With a hint of pepper and slightly tangy flavor, this barbecue spectacular will impress even those who don't include fish among their favorite foods.

1-1/2 lb	monkfish	750 g
1	lime, quartered	1
1	small lemon, quartered	1
MARINADE:		
1/4 cup	lime juice	50 mL
1/4 cup	vegetable oil	50 mL
4 tsp	Worcestershire sauce	20 mL
1	small onion, minced	1
2	cloves garlic, minced	2
1-1/2 tsp	ground cumin	7 mL
1 tsp	grated lime rind	5 mL
1/4 tsp	pepper	1 mL

- **Marinade:** In large glass bowl, whisk together lime juice, oil, Worcestershire sauce, onion, garlic, cumin, lime rind and pepper; set aside.
- Cut monkfish into 1-1/2-inch (4 cm) chunks; add to marinade, tossing to coat. Cover and refrigerate for 30 minutes.
- Remove monkfish from marinade, reserving marinade. On each of 4 greased metal skewers, thread 2 pieces of fish followed by lime quarter, 2 pieces of fish followed by lemon quarter, then 2 pieces of fish.
- Cook brochettes on greased grill over medium-hot coals or on medium setting, turning twice and basting occasionally with marinade, for 10 to 12 minutes or until fish flakes easily when tested with fork. Makes 4 to 6 servings.

HERBED SWORDFISH STEAKS

Serve these easy steaks with grilled tomato slices drizzled with olive oil. For a new twist, substitute shark for swordfish.

1/4 cup	minced fresh parsley	50 mL
1/4 cup	olive oil	50 mL
2 tbsp	lemon juice	25 mL
2	cloves garlic, minced	2
1 tbsp	chopped fresh oregano (or 1 tsp/ 5 mL dried)	15 mL
2 tsp	Dijon mustard	10 mL
1/2 tsp	chopped fresh thyme (or 1/4 tsp/ 1 mL dried)	2 mL
1/2 tsp	pepper	2 mL
1-1/2 lb	swordfish or shark steak (3/4 inch/ 2 cm thick)	750 g
	Salt	

• In shallow dish large enough to hold steaks in single layer, mix together parsley, oil, lemon juice, garlic, oregano, mustard, thyme and pepper. Add steaks, turning to coat well; cover and marinate for 30 minutes at room temperature or 1 hour in refrigerator, turning often.

• Remove steaks, reserving any marinade. Cook on greased grill over hot coals or on high setting for 3 to 4 minutes or until steaks are well marked. Turning carefully and brushing lightly with marinade, cook for 3 to 4 minutes longer or until fish flakes easily when tested with fork. Season with salt to taste. Makes 4 servings.

GRILLED GARLICKY SMELT

When purchasing smelt for the barbecue, choose the largest ones available, 4 to 5 inches (10 to 12 cm) long. Keep a spray bottle of water nearby to douse any flare-ups.

1-1/4 lb	smelt	625 g
1/2 cup	all-purpose flour	125 mL
1 tsp	salt	5 mL
1/4 cup	butter, melted	50 mL
2 tbsp	vegetable oil	25 mL
1	clove garlic, minced	1
	Pepper	
	Lemon wedges	

• Rinse smelt under cold running water; drain well. Place flour and salt in plastic bag; add smelt, a few at a time, shaking to coat well.

• Mix together butter, oil, garlic, and pepper to taste. Place smelt on greased wire rack. Brush with butter mixture. Top with second greased wire rack.

• Holding racks together, turn over and cook smelt, buttered sides down, over hot coals or on high setting, basting frequently with butter mixture, for 5 minutes. Turn over and cook for 4 to 6 minutes longer or until smelt are crispy on the outside and flake easily when tested with fork. Serve with lemon wedges. Makes about 4 servings.

BARBECUING FISH

• *Compensate for the lack of natural fat in fish by using marinades and basting sauces to prevent drying out. These can be as simple as lemon juice and oil or melted butter. Add flavor and color with fresh garden herbs.*

• *Fish is naturally tender and tends to break easily when cooked so handle it carefully when serving.*

• *Oil barbecue surfaces, especially if cooking fish directly on grill. Baste fish frequently and keep a glass of water nearby to douse flare-ups when basting oils hit coals.*

• *Use a greased wire fish basket for whole or split fish. Alternatively, oil one side of a double piece of heavy foil that is at least as long as the fish and 2-1/2 times as wide; punch numerous pencil-size holes in foil and place, oiled side up, on greased grill. Place whole fish slightly off-centre on foil. Halfway through cooking time, fold foil over fish, flip package and re-open to complete cooking. Or use the grill-poaching foil method (see Grill-Poached Stuffed Pickerel, page 83).*

• *Don't overcook fish. Winds and outside temperatures will affect cooking time but a general rule is to barbecue fish over hot coals or at high setting for 10 minutes per inch (2.5 cm) of thickness, measured at thickest point of fish.*

Marinades and Sauces

Piquant sauces help bring out the rich smoky tastes of barbecuing. Choose a zesty marinade to tenderize and add flavor before cooking, a basting sauce or glaze to brush on food while cooking, or a sauce to accompany the finished dish. Here are a variety of recipes and tips to see you through a summer of barbecuing.

JAPANESE TERIYAKI MARINADE

This is particularly delicious for salmon steaks, scallop kabobs, chicken, chicken livers and beef steaks. A popular Japanese appetizer is yakitori, made with small pieces of marinated chicken and chicken livers threaded on skewers and grilled.

1/2 cup	light soy sauce	125 mL
1/2 cup	Japanese cooking wine (mirin)*	125 mL
1/3 cup	granulated sugar	75 mL
1	clove garlic, smashed and left whole	1
1	piece (1 inch/2.5 cm) gingerroot, cut in half	1

• In small saucepan, combine soy sauce, Japanese cooking wine, sugar, garlic and gingerroot; bring to boil and cook for a few minutes or until syrupy. Remove from heat; discard garlic and ginger. Let cool.
• Marinate food in about 3/4 cup (175 mL) sauce for 20 minutes. When ready to cook food, reheat remaining marinade and brush over food several times during cooking and once again at end of cooking to glaze. Makes 1-1/2 cups (375 mL).
*Available in Japanese food stores.

HOT AND SPICY MARINADE

This marinade is terrific for ribs, pork chops, pork tenderloin and pork roasts such as loin and butt.

1 cup	ketchup	250 mL
1 cup	chili sauce	250 mL
1/4 cup	vegetable oil	50 mL
1/4 cup	Dijon mustard	50 mL
1/4 cup	lemon juice	50 mL
2 tbsp	Worcestershire sauce	25 mL
1 tbsp	hot Chinese chili paste (optional)*	15 mL
2 tsp	hot pepper sauce	10 mL
1 tsp	hot pepper flakes	5 mL
1/2 tsp	pepper	2 mL
3	cloves garlic, minced	3
1	onion, minced	1

• Combine ketchup, chili sauce, oil, mustard, lemon juice, Worcestershire sauce, hot Chinese chili paste (if using), hot pepper sauce and flakes, pepper, garlic and onion; mix well. Makes 3 cups (750 mL).
*Available in oriental and specialty food stores.

Hot and Spicy Marinade;
Japanese Teriyaki Marinade

Marinades and Sauces   93

Basting chicken on the grill

LEMON-ROSEMARY MARINADE

Try this marinade with lamb, chicken, veal roasts, pork and fish.

1/2 cup	lemon juice	125 mL
1/2 cup	dry white wine	125 mL
1/2 cup	olive oil	125 mL
2 tbsp	chopped fresh rosemary (or 1 tsp/ 5 mL dried)	25 mL
2 tbsp	chopped fresh parsley	25 mL
1 tsp	grated lemon rind	5 mL
1/2 tsp	salt	2 mL
1/4 tsp	pepper	1 mL
1	bay leaf, broken in thirds	1

• Combine lemon juice, wine, oil, rosemary, parsley, lemon rind, salt, pepper and bay leaf; mix well. Makes 2 cups (500 mL).

MUSTARD PEPPERCORN MARINADE

Use this rich, spicy marinade to bring out the flavor of beef. This makes enough for 2 lb (1 kg) of steak.

1 tsp	mustard seeds	5 mL
1 tsp	black peppercorns	5 mL
1 tbsp	Dijon mustard	15 mL
1/4 cup	dry red wine	50 mL
2 tbsp	vegetable oil	25 mL

• With mortar and pestle or in plastic bag with rolling pin, crush mustard seeds and peppercorns. Blend in mustard; stir in wine and oil. Spread all over meat; cover and marinate at room temperature for 2 hours or overnight in refrigerator. Makes about 1/2 cup (125 mL) marinade.

MARINATING TIPS

• *Place the food to be marinated inside a plastic bag and set bag in a large pan or baking dish. Pour in marinade, press out air, tie bag securely and refrigerate. Turn the bag occasionally to coat food thoroughly. Alternatively, use a glass or ceramic container.*
• *The tougher and larger the cut of meat, the longer it needs to be marinated.*

BEEF

• *Less tender cuts of beef, such as blade roasts or short ribs, should be marinated for 24 to 48 hours to make them more tender. For moist, flavorful, tender results, marinate flank or round steak for 24 hours before barbecuing.*
• *Marinate tender cuts, such as sirloin steak or prime rib roast, for 1 to 24 hours to change the flavor. The longer meat marinates, the greater the flavor change.*

ALL-PURPOSE BASTING SAUCE

This sauce adds zip to the season's barbecuing. It will keep for several weeks in the refrigerator and is delicious when basted on steak, chicken and ribs during the last few minutes of grilling.

1 cup	ketchup	250 mL
1/2 cup	packed brown sugar	125 mL
1/2 cup	chili sauce	125 mL
1/2 cup	cider vinegar	125 mL
2 tbsp	prepared mustard	25 mL
2 tbsp	vegetable oil	25 mL
1 tbsp	Worcestershire sauce	15 mL
2	cloves garlic, minced	2
Dash	hot pepper sauce	Dash

• In saucepan, stir together ketchup, sugar, chili sauce, vinegar, mustard, oil, Worcestershire sauce, garlic and hot pepper sauce; bring to boil. Remove from heat and stir well. Let stand for 30 minutes before using.
• Refrigerate cooled sauce in covered jar for up to 3 weeks. Makes 2 1/2 cups (625 mL) sauce.

RED HOT BARBECUE BASTING SAUCE

Keep this delicious sauce on hand to become the "house" sauce for the last few minutes of grilling time for meat and chicken. It's also great as a zesty condiment. Store cooled sauce in covered jar in refrigerator for up to 3 weeks.

2 tbsp	olive oil	25 mL
1	onion, minced	1
2	cloves garlic, minced	2
1	can (5-1/2 oz/156 mL) tomato paste	1
2	tomatoes, peeled, seeded and minced	2
1-1/2 cups	water	375 mL
1/2 cup	red wine	125 mL
1/3 cup	Worcestershire sauce	75 mL
1/4 cup	red wine vinegar	50 mL
3 tbsp	packed brown sugar	50 mL
1 tsp	dry mustard	5 mL
1 tsp	crushed hot pepper flakes	5 mL
3/4 tsp	ground cumin	4 mL
1/4 tsp	cayenne pepper	1 mL
1/4 tsp	ground coriander	1 mL

• In saucepan, heat oil over low heat; cook onion and garlic until softened, about 10 minutes.
• Stir in tomato paste, tomatoes, water, wine, Worcestershire sauce, vinegar, sugar, mustard, hot pepper flakes, cumin, cayenne and coriander; simmer, uncovered, for 30 minutes, stirring occasionally. Makes about 3 cups (750 mL) sauce.

PORK

• *Marinate pork chops for 1 to 24 hours to add extra flavor before grilling.*
• *Precook spareribs in simmering water for 30 minutes, then marinate for up to 48 hours. This allows some of the fat to drain off and prevents ribs from drying out during cooking. Because of the precooking, marinated spareribs only need 10 to 15 minutes on the barbecue.*

LAMB

• *Because lamb leg and ribs are usually tender to begin with, marinate for 4 hours or more to change flavor, then barbecue.*

SEAFOOD

• *Marinate fish for 1 to 24 hours for greater flavor. Barbecue for 10 minutes for every 1 inch (2.5 cm) of thickness of fish.*
• *Scallops can be marinated for 1 to 4 hours.*

TEXAS-STYLE BASTING SAUCE

Superb barbecued chicken is a cinch when you have this basting sauce on hand. Add a pinch of basil and thyme to the sauce if you like extra flavor.

2 tbsp	vegetable oil	25 mL
1	large onion, minced	1
2	cloves garlic, minced	2
1	can (5-1/2 oz/156 mL) tomato paste	1
1 cup	water	250 mL
1/4 cup	packed brown sugar	50 mL
1/4 cup	vinegar	50 mL
2 tbsp	Worcestershire sauce	25 mL
1 tbsp	Dijon mustard	15 mL
1/4 tsp	pepper	1 mL
	Salt	
	Hot pepper sauce	

• In heavy saucepan, heat oil over medium heat; cook onion and garlic until tender. Add tomato paste, water, sugar, vinegar, Worcestershire sauce, mustard, pepper, and salt and hot pepper sauce to taste; mix well. Bring to boil; reduce heat and simmer for 5 minutes.

• Use warm, or let cool, cover and refrigerate for up to 1 week. Transfer some of the sauce to small dish and use to brush over chicken during last 5 to 10 minutes of cooking. Makes about 2 cups (500 mL) sauce, enough for about six 3-lb (1.5 kg) chickens.

TANGY TOMATO SAUCE

This sauce is delicious with any cut of beef—steak, thick slices of roast beef, thin slices of marinated flank steak or hamburgers. To baste meat with this sauce during cooking, remember that tomato chars easily, so use it only during the last five minutes of cooking. Store the sauce, covered, in your refrigerator for up to 2 weeks.

1	can (7-1/2 oz/213 mL) tomato sauce	1
1/2 cup	red wine	125 mL
1/4 cup	tomato paste	50 mL
2 tbsp	tarragon vinegar	25 mL
1 tbsp	packed brown sugar	15 mL
1/2 tsp	dried oregano	2 mL
1/4 tsp	each salt, dried thyme and basil	1 mL
1	clove garlic, crushed	1
2 or 3	drops hot pepper sauce	2 or 3

• In small saucepan, combine tomato sauce, wine, tomato paste, vinegar, sugar, oregano, salt, thyme, basil, garlic and hot pepper sauce. Bring just to boil; remove from heat. Makes 1-1/4 cups (375 mL).

MARINADES

A marinade is usually a thin sauce containing some type of acid such as citrus juice, vinegar, wine or yogurt to tenderize the meat, as well as herbs, spices or vegetables to add flavor. If the sauce is to be used later for basting, it will probably contain oil to prevent food from drying during the barbecuing.

BASTING SAUCES

A basting sauce can be as simple as an herb-flavored oil or melted butter to brush on foods such as meats, fish, poultry and vegetables. Basting prevents food from drying out while cooking and adds flavor.

Thicker basting sauces for meat often have a high sugar content; they should be used during the last few minutes of cooking to avoid burning the food yet still give it an appetizing glaze.

If the meat has been marinated in a sauce with a high sugar content that's to be used later for basting, keep the grill four to six inches (10 to 15 cm) from the coals or use a lower temperature on a gas or electric barbecue throughout the whole cooking period so the meat doesn't burn before it's cooked through.

ACCOMPANYING SAUCES

Remember that familiar sauces like bearnaise, hollandaise and sweet-and-sour are just as delicious with barbecued

Ginger Orange Sauce

foods as they are with foods cooked indoors.

Whatever its role, the sauce should complement but never dominate the flavor of the food. Highly spiced or tart sauces go well with beef and lamb; sweet-and-sour flavors are good with ham, pork and poultry. Fish and vegetables require light sauces.

GINGER ORANGE SAUCE

This delicious sweet sauce is ideal for chicken, turkey and pork. Use it simply to baste during the last few minutes of grilling, or use as a marinade before grilling and basting.

1/3 cup	orange marmalade (preferably Seville)	75 mL
1/4 cup	soy sauce	50 mL
2 tbsp	lemon juice	25 mL
2	cloves garlic, minced	2
1 tbsp	grated fresh gingerroot	15 mL
	Salt and pepper	

• In small saucepan, stir together marmalade, soy sauce, lemon juice, garlic, gingerroot, and salt and pepper to taste; bring to boil. Remove from heat and stir well. Let cool to room temperature if using as marinade. Makes 3/4 cup (175 mL) sauce.

BEER BARBECUE SAUCE

This is a fabulous marinade-sauce for barbecued spareribs, pork chops or chicken. Parboil ribs for 45 minutes before marinating to release fat and make them tender.

1 cup	prepared barbecue sauce	250 mL
1 cup	ketchup	250 mL
2/3 cup	beer	150 mL
1/4 cup	honey or molasses	50 mL
2 tbsp	lemon juice	25 mL
2 tbsp	red wine vinegar	25 mL
2 tbsp	Dijon mustard	25 mL
1 tbsp	Worcestershire sauce	15 mL
1 tsp	hot pepper sauce	5 mL
1/2 tsp	pepper	2 mL
2	cloves garlic, minced	2
2	onions, finely chopped	2

• In large bowl, combine barbecue sauce, ketchup, beer, honey, lemon juice, vinegar, mustard, Worcestershire sauce, hot pepper sauce, pepper, garlic and onions.
• Place food in marinade and let stand at room temperature for up to 2 hours or in refrigerator overnight.
• When ready to cook, remove food and place marinade in saucepan and cook for 10 minutes or until thickened. Use as sauce for basting or serving with cooked food. Makes about 3 cups (750 mL).

The same rule applies to cooking with beer as with wine: Use the kind of beer you enjoy drinking. If you prefer a mild ale, use it to give food a mild flavor. If you prefer a malty, heartier effect, use a "stout" or rich-flavored beer. You can use flat beer for cooking, so if you have opened bottles in the refrigerator, use them up in food preparation. Use beer to tenderize tough cuts of meat.

HONEY GARLIC SAUCE

This piquant sweet-and-sour sauce is good for basting pork roasts or chops during grilling. Or marinate chops in it for two hours, then brush sauce over chops at the end of the grilling time.

1/4 cup	vegetable oil	50 mL
1/4 cup	lemon juice	50 mL
2 tbsp	soy sauce	25 mL
2 tbsp	liquid honey	25 mL
2	cloves garlic, minced	2

• In small bowl, stir together oil, lemon juice, soy sauce, honey and garlic. Makes 3/4 cup (175 mL) sauce.

Fireworks Barbecue Sauce makes a great topping for hamburgers, and can also be used as a marinade to tenderize economical medium-tender cuts. To make the marinade: Combine equal parts of Fireworks Barbecue Sauce (puréed smooth, if desired) and vegetable oil. Marinate chuck, blade, cross rib, round or sirloin tip steaks for 8 to 12 hours in the refrigerator, flank steak for up to 24 hours. Most of these cuts are best grilled just to medium doneness; flank steak should be grilled quickly just to rare or medium-rare. To serve, slice the meat thinly on the diagonal across the grain.

FIREWORKS BARBECUE SAUCE

This sauce can be chunky or smooth, mild or red-hot; divide it into variations as desired. For a fiery sauce, add a dash of cayenne or hot pepper sauce, a small hot pepper (finely minced) or hot pepper flakes after 30 minutes of cooking. (photo, p.23)

1/4 cup	vegetable oil	50 mL
2 cups	finely chopped onions	500 mL
1/2 cup	finely chopped sweet green pepper	125 mL
1/2 cup	finely chopped celery	125 mL
2	cloves garlic, minced	2
1	can (28 oz/796 mL) plum tomatoes	1
1 cup	ketchup	250 mL
1	can (5-1/2 oz/156 mL) tomato paste	1
1/4 cup	packed brown sugar or honey	50 mL
1/4 cup	cider vinegar	50 mL
1/4 cup	Worcestershire sauce	50 mL
1	can (10 oz/284 mL) beef broth	1
1 tbsp	chili powder	15 mL
1 tsp	cumin	5 mL
1 tsp	salt	5 mL
1/2 tsp	pepper	2 mL
1/2 tsp	dried oregano	2 mL
1/2 tsp	allspice	2 mL
1	bay leaf	1

• In large heavy saucepan, heat oil; cook onions, green pepper, celery and garlic until softened, without browning. Add tomatoes, crushing to break up. Stir in ketchup, tomato paste, sugar, vinegar, Worcestershire sauce, beef broth, chili powder, cumin, salt, pepper, oregano, allspice and bay leaf.
• Bring to gentle boil. Simmer, uncovered, for 45 minutes or until desired thickness, stirring often. Discard bay leaf. Purée sauce if desired. Store covered in refrigerator. Makes about 6 cups (1.5 L).

Vegetables and Salads

Everyone loves the crisp fresh tastes of summery salads. Because most salads can be partially prepared in advance, you and the kitchen can keep cool until it's time to dine. Salads are ideal for entertaining so try a simple tossed salad with a classic vinaigrette or one of our stunning composed salads or salad platters.

The barbecue isn't just for meat! Here you'll find recipes and tips for grilling a wide variety of vegetables—from traditional grilled potatoes and corn-on-the-cob to cherry tomatoes, red onions and vegetable kabobs.

ROMANOFF FRUIT SALAD

Traditional Strawberries Romanoff is made by marinating strawberries in orange juice and orange liqueur, then topping them with sweetened whipped cream. This version drizzles an orange-flavored sauce over fresh seasonal fruit and a protein food, such as Swiss cheese, cottage cheese or cooked chicken breast. Serve with melba toast.

1	bunch red-tipped lettuce	1
2 cups	strawberries, hulled	500 mL
2 cups	red cherries, pitted	500 mL
1 cup	raspberries	250 mL
1/2 cup	red currants	125 mL
	Cottage cheese, Swiss cheese or cooked chicken breast	
DRESSING:		
1/4 cup	red currant jelly	50 mL
1 cup	sour cream or plain yogurt	250 mL
1/4 cup	orange juice	50 mL
1 tsp	grated orange rind	5 mL

- **Dressing:** In small heavy saucepan, melt jelly over low heat. Pour into bowl; let cool slightly, then whisk in sour cream, orange juice and rind. Refrigerate until chilled.
- To assemble salad, place lettuce leaves on individual plates. Arrange strawberries, cherries, raspberries, currants and cottage cheese attractively on top. Pass dressing separately. Makes 4 to 6 servings.

(Clockwise from top) Sushi Salad (p. 102); Salade Naturelle (p. 105); Romanoff Fruit Salad

SUSHI SALAD

Here, sushi rice is combined with seafood and a colorful assortment of vegetables. If radish or pepper sprouts are unavailable, use watercress, torn into bite-sized pieces; it has the same peppery taste. (photo, p.100)

	Seasoned Sushi Rice (recipe opposite page)	
1/2 lb	cooked crab meat	250 g
1 cup	cooked julienned carrots	250 mL
1 cup	cooked peas	250 mL
1/4 cup	chopped fresh dill	50 mL
2 cups	radish or pepper sprouts	500 mL
6	green onions, finely diced	6

DRESSING:

1/3 cup	soy sauce	75 mL
3 tbsp	rice vinegar	50 mL
2 tbsp	granulated sugar	25 mL
1 tbsp	finely chopped gingerroot	15 mL
1 tbsp	sesame oil	15 mL

GARNISH:

	Enoki mushrooms (optional)	
2 tbsp	sesame seeds, toasted*	25 mL

• **Dressing:** Whisk together soy sauce, vinegar, sugar, gingerroot and sesame oil. Set aside.
• In bowl, combine Seasoned Sushi Rice, crab meat, carrots, peas and dill. Toss gently with just enough dressing to moisten.
• In separate bowl, toss together radish sprouts and onions with enough of the remaining dressing to moisten.
• To assemble salad, arrange radish sprout mixture around border of serving platter. Mound rice mixture in centre.
• **Garnish:** Sprinkle salad with mushrooms (if using) and sesame seeds. Pass remaining dressing separately. Makes 4 to 6 servings.
*Toast sesame seeds in dry skillet over medium-high heat, stirring, for about 1 minute or until golden.

Summer Garden Salad

SUMMER GARDEN SALAD

• *Mix and match contrasting colors, textures and flavors to create beautiful salad plates.*
• *Attractively arrange radicchio, leaf lettuces, Belgian endive, dandelion greens, mâche (lamb's lettuce), chervil, Italian parsley, sorrel, cucumber, oyster mushrooms, yellow pear tomatoes, fresh figs and violets.*
• *Make this a complete supper with the addition of cheese—we used goat cheese—cut into shapes and rolled in coarsely ground pepper. Drizzle with a light vinaigrette.*

SEASONED SUSHI RICE:

1-1/2 cups	short-grain Japanese rice	375 mL
1-3/4 cups	cold water	425 mL
1/3 cup	seasoned rice vinegar	75 mL

• Rinse rice under cold running water until water runs clear. In heavy saucepan with tight-fitting lid, combine rice with cold water. Let stand for 15 minutes. Cover and bring to boil; boil for 5 minutes. Reduce heat to medium and cook until water is absorbed, about 5 minutes.

• To dry rice, increase heat to high and cook for 30 seconds. Remove from heat and let stand for 10 minutes. Transfer rice to large bowl. While fanning with fan or piece of cardboard, gradually sprinkle vinegar over rice and toss with paddle or wooden spoon. Do not refrigerate. Rice will keep at room temperature for 4 to 6 hours. Makes about 3 cups (750 mL).

MARINATED SEAFOOD AND SNOW PEA SALAD

This delicious chilled salad is perfect for hot summer days.

1/2 lb	scallops	250 g
1/2 cup	water	125 mL
1/4 cup	dry vermouth or water	50 mL
2 cups	snow peas, trimmed	500 mL
1 lb	peeled deveined cooked large shrimp	500 g
10	cherry tomatoes, cut in half	10
	Leaf or Bibb lettuce leaves	

LEMON-MUSTARD MARINADE:

1/2 cup	vegetable oil	125 mL
3 tbsp	lemon juice	50 mL
2 tbsp	chopped fresh chives or green onions	25 mL
2 tbsp	chopped fresh basil or fresh dill	25 mL
1 tsp	dry mustard	5 mL
1/2 tsp	granulated sugar	2 mL
1/2 tsp	grated lemon rind	2 mL
1	small clove garlic, minced	1
	Salt and pepper	

Salmon, halibut, shark or any firm-fleshed fish fillets or steaks may be substituted for scallops and shrimp in Marinated Seafood and Snow Pea Salad. Simply poach the fish until barely opaque and let cool in poaching liquid. Drain; cut into chunks, removing bones. Alternatively, barbecue fish on grill over hot coals or on high setting. Refrigerate until ready to marinate for the salad.

• In small saucepan, combine scallops, water and vermouth. Bring to boil, stirring occasionally; cook for about 2 minutes or until scallops are opaque. Drain and set aside.

• In pot of boiling water, blanch snow peas for 30 seconds or just until tender-crisp. Drain and refresh under cold running water; drain again. Cover and refrigerate while making marinade.

• **Lemon-Mustard Marinade:** In large bowl, whisk together oil, lemon juice, chives, basil, mustard, sugar, lemon rind, garlic, and salt and pepper to taste until well blended. Add shrimp and scallops; stir to coat well. Cover and refrigerate for 1 hour.

• Just before serving, toss snow peas and tomatoes with seafood mixture. Line serving dish with lettuce leaves. Using slotted spoon, mound seafood mixture on top. Makes 4 to 6 servings.

SUMMER FRUIT SALAD PLATTER

Light and luscious, this refreshing combination of fresh fruits and seasonal mixed greens makes a perfect main course on a hot summer day.

1	pineapple	1
Half	cantaloupe	Half
2	grapefruit, peeled and sectioned	2
1-1/2 cups	seedless green grapes	375 mL
2	apples, cored and diced	2
1	small head romaine lettuce	1
1	head Boston lettuce	1
2 cups	loosely packed fresh spinach	500 mL
1/2 lb	prosciutto or smoked ham, julienned	250 g
	Strawberries or raspberries (optional)	

RASPBERRY VINEGAR DRESSING:

1/2 cup	raspberry vinegar	125 mL
1/4 cup	vegetable oil	50 mL
1/4 cup	liquid honey	50 mL
1 tbsp	lime juice	15 mL

• Quarter pineapple lengthwise; core and cube, then place in large bowl. Using melon baller, scoop out cantaloupe. Add to bowl along with grapefruit, grapes and apples; combine gently.

• Tear romaine, Boston lettuce and spinach into bite-sized pieces; combine in separate bowl.

• **Raspberry Vinegar Dressing:** Whisk together vinegar, oil, honey and lime juice; pour over mixed greens and toss. Add prosciutto and half of the fruit; toss gently. Spread evenly on large platter; attractively arrange remaining fruit in centre. Garnish with strawberries (if using). Makes about 8 servings.

Summer Fruit Salad Platter

RICE AND ASPARAGUS SALAD

At the height of asparagus season, serve this piquant lemon- and garlic-dressed salad.

3/4 cup	parboiled long-grain rice	175 mL
1-1/2 cups	boiling salted water	375 mL
3/4 lb	asparagus spears	375 g
1/2 cup	diced sweet yellow or green pepper	125 mL
1/4 cup	diced red onion	50 mL
1/2 tsp	grated lemon rind	2 mL
2 tbsp	lemon juice	25 mL
1 tbsp	Dijon mustard	15 mL
1	clove garlic, minced	1
1/2 tsp	salt	2 mL
1/4 tsp	pepper	1 mL
1/4 cup	vegetable oil	50 mL

• In saucepan, add rice to boiling salted water; reduce heat and simmer, covered, until water is absorbed and rice is tender, about 20 minutes. Fluff with fork; transfer to bowl.
• Meanwhile, trim asparagus; cut on diagonal into 1-inch (2.5 cm) lengths. Cook, covered, in boiling water until tender-crisp, about 4 minutes. Drain; refresh under cold running water. Drain again and pat dry. Add to rice. Add yellow pepper and onion.
• In separate bowl, stir together lemon rind and juice, mustard, garlic, salt and pepper; whisk in oil. Drizzle over rice mixture, tossing gently. Taste and adjust seasoning. Makes about 4 servings.

SALADE NATURELLE

This beautiful salad will be popular with those trying to cut down on fats because the dressing is made without oil. Smoked chicken can be replaced with cold barbecued chicken. (photo, p.100)

1	head Boston lettuce	1
2	Belgian endives	2
8	bunches lamb's lettuce (mâche)	8
1 lb	fresh asparagus, cooked	500 g
1 lb	smoked chicken or turkey, julienned	500 g
DRESSING:		
1	cucumber	1
1 tsp	salt	5 mL
1-1/2 cups	plain yogurt	375 mL
2 tbsp	chopped fresh tarragon (or 1/2 tsp/2 mL dried)	25 mL
1 tsp	prepared horseradish	5 mL
1/2 tsp	Dijon mustard	2 mL
	Pepper	
GARNISH (optional):		
	Cucumber twists	
	Radish roses	

• **Dressing:** Peel, seed and grate cucumber. Sprinkle with salt and toss well. Place in colander and let stand for 30 minutes. Rinse, drain well and squeeze dry. Set aside.
• In bowl, whisk together yogurt, tarragon, horseradish, mustard, and pepper to taste. Stir in cucumber. Taste and adjust seasoning if necessary. Refrigerate until chilled.
• To assemble salad, line 4 large plates with Boston lettuce leaves. Arrange endive leaves in circle with tips pointing to edge of plate. Arrange lamb's lettuce leaves inside endives. Arrange asparagus like spokes of wheel; arrange chicken between spokes. Spoon some dressing over each salad.
• **Garnish:** Arrange cucumber twists and radish roses (if using) on each plate. Pass remaining dressing separately. Makes 4 servings.

FRUIT VINEGARS

Substitute any fruit vinegar for the raspberry vinegar called for in Summer Fruit Salad Platter. To make your own fruit vinegar, simply place 1 cup (250 mL) washed raspberries, strawberries, blueberries, red or black currants, or chopped peeled peaches or plums in a 2-cup (500 mL) sterilized Mason-type jar. Fill with plain white vinegar and seal. Let stand in a dark place for 2 to 3 weeks. Strain vinegar into sterilized jar and seal. Store in a cool dry place. Makes about 1 cup (250 mL).

SPINACH SALAD WITH LEMON SOY DRESSING

This hint-of-the-Orient dressing is great on spinach.

4	thin slices red onion	4
4	black olives	4
1	orange	1
8 cups	lightly packed trimmed spinach	2 L
1 tbsp	lemon juice	15 mL
2 tsp	dry white wine or chicken stock	10 mL
1 tsp	light soy sauce	5 mL
1/4 tsp	granulated sugar	1 mL
Pinch	pepper	Pinch
Dash	hot pepper sauce	Dash
2 tbsp	vegetable oil	25 mL

• Separate red onion slices into rings. Quarter olives, discarding pits. Peel orange; using sharp knife, remove membranes from orange sections. Arrange spinach in salad bowl. Top with onion rings, olive quarters and orange sections.
• In small bowl, stir together lemon juice, wine, soy sauce, sugar, pepper and hot pepper sauce; whisk in oil. Drizzle over salad; toss. Taste and adjust seasoning. Makes about 4 servings.

MELON AND SHRIMP SALAD WITH THAI DRESSING

Flavorful, peanutty dressing loaded with the fresh taste of coriander then drizzled over fruit and seafood makes an intriguing luncheon plate.

1	cantaloupe, cut in 12 wedges and peeled	1
1 lb	seedless green grapes	500 g
1	head Boston lettuce, inner leaves only	1
12	cooked jumbo shrimp	12
DRESSING:		
1/3 cup	vegetable oil	75 mL
1/3 cup	lime juice	75 mL
2	cloves garlic, minced	2
1 tbsp	minced gingerroot	15 mL
2 tbsp	peanut butter	25 mL
2	green onions, minced	2
1/2 cup	chopped fresh coriander	125 mL
1 tbsp	packed brown sugar	15 mL
Pinch	(approx) hot pepper flakes	Pinch

• **Dressing:** In food processor, combine oil, lime juice, garlic and gingerroot. Add peanut butter, onions, coriander, sugar and hot pepper flakes, adding more hot pepper flakes if desired; process just until combined.
• On 4 salad plates, attractively arrange cantaloupe, grapes, lettuce and shrimp. Spoon a little dressing over each salad. Serve remaining dressing separately. Makes 4 servings.

Spinach Salad with Lemon Soy Dressing and Melon and Shrimp Salad with Thai Dressing are both salads that can easily be doubled and are great to carry to potluck suppers or to make ahead for patio parties. Simply prepare salad ingredients and arrange in bowl or on platters; cover and refrigerate until serving time. Mix salad dressing and refrigerate in small jar with tight-fitting lid. At mealtime, shake dressing and drizzle over salad.

*Fruit Salad with Turkey;
Melon and Shrimp Salad
with Thai Dressing*

FRUIT SALAD WITH TURKEY

*This easy salad is a great make-ahead meal.
While the turkey is chilling in the wine cooking
liquid, make the dressing ahead to allow the
flavors to mingle. Then, just before serving, all
you have to do is arrange the salad attractively
on the plates.*

1/2 cup	dry white wine	125 mL
1-3/4 lb	boneless skinless turkey breast	875 g
1	bunch leaf lettuce, separated	1
DRESSING:		
1/4 cup	orange juice	50 mL
1/4 cup	white wine vinegar	50 mL
2 tsp	Dijon mustard	10 mL
2 tsp	liquid honey	10 mL
1/2 tsp	grated orange rind	2 mL
3/4 cup	vegetable oil	175 mL
	Salt and pepper	
GARNISH:		
	Sliced nectarines	
	Sliced English cucumber	
	Seedless red grapes	
	Toasted sliced almonds	

• In 8-cup (2 L) microwaveable casserole or
square baking dish, pour wine over turkey;
cover with lid or vented plastic wrap and
microwave at High for 5 minutes. Turn turkey
over; microwave at Medium (50%) for 15 to
20 minutes longer or until juices run clear
when turkey is pierced with skewer and meat
thermometer registers 185°F (85°C), turning
turkey over and rotating dish twice.
• Let stand for 10 minutes; refrigerate turkey
in cooking liquid until chilled or overnight.
Drain and slice thinly.
• **Dressing:** Whisk together orange juice,
vinegar, mustard, honey and orange rind;
gradually whisk in oil. Season with salt and
pepper to taste.
• **Garnish:** Line salad plates with lettuce.
Arrange sliced turkey on top. Garnish plates
with nectarines, cucumber, grapes and
almonds. Drizzle with just enough dressing to
moisten each salad. Makes 6 to 8 servings.

SHRIMP AND AVOCADO PLATTER

Shrimp and Avocado Platter

Use your imagination in presenting this luscious salad to eager diners. Serve it in individual avocado shells or mound the salad on a lettuce-lined platter. Either way, garnish it with a few slices of avocado brushed with lemon juice.

4	ripe avocados	4
4	tomatoes, seeded and chopped	4
4 cups	cooked salad shrimp (about 1 lb/ 500 g)	1 L
1 cup	finely chopped English cucumber or diced celery	250 mL
1/2 cup	chopped fresh parsley	125 mL
2 tbsp	chopped fresh mint	25 mL
	Lemon juice (optional)	
	Leaf lettuce	
	Mint leaves or watercress	

TOMATO FRENCH DRESSING:		
1/3 cup	vegetable oil	75 mL
1/4 cup	ketchup	50 mL
2 tbsp	white wine vinegar	25 mL
2 tbsp	lemon juice	25 mL
1 tsp	Worcestershire sauce	5 mL
1 tsp	granulated sugar	5 mL
1/4 tsp	dry mustard	1 mL
	Pepper	

• Halve and pit avocados. Scoop out pulp; dice and place in large bowl along with tomatoes, shrimp, cucumber, parsley and mint. (If using avocado shells, brush with lemon juice and set aside.)

• **Tomato French Dressing:** Combine oil, ketchup, vinegar, lemon juice, Worcestershire sauce, sugar, mustard, and pepper to taste; mix until well blended. Pour over salad and toss gently to mix.

• Mound salad on lettuce-lined platter or in avocado shells. Garnish with mint leaves. Makes 8 servings.

CAULIFLOWER AND RED PEPPER SALAD

This salad can be prepared well in advance and makes a colorful addition to a buffet table, barbecue or brunch menu. (photo, p.71)

1	large cauliflower	1
1	large sweet red pepper, roasted and cut in strips*	1
2	heads radicchio or Belgian endives, separated in leaves	2
6	hard-cooked eggs, quartered	6

DRESSING:

1 tsp	granulated sugar	5 mL
3/4 tsp	salt	4 mL
1/2 tsp	pepper	2 mL
	Juice and grated rind of 1 lemon	
1	onion, finely chopped	1
2	cloves garlic, minced	2
1/2 cup	olive oil	125 mL

• In pot of boiling salted water, cook cauliflower until tender-crisp, about 5 minutes. Drain and let cool slightly. Separate into florets and place in large deep bowl along with roasted red pepper strips.

• **Dressing:** In screw-top jar or mixing bowl, combine sugar, salt, pepper, lemon juice, rind, onion, garlic and oil; shake or mix well. Pour over warm salad. Cover and chill for at least 3 hours or overnight.

• At serving time, line salad bowl with radicchio. Drain cauliflower and red pepper, reserving dressing; spoon vegetables over radicchio. Pour dressing over and garnish with egg quarters around edge of bowl. Makes 6 to 8 servings.

*Broil red pepper for about 4 minutes per side or until charred all over. Remove from oven and place in plastic bag; let steam for 10 minutes, then peel, seed and cut into strips.

PLATTER PRESENTATION

Perfect as a barbecue accompaniment, a salad platter is the answer to enjoyable warm-weather cooking.

• *Use the edge of the plate as a picture frame. Keep salad and greens off the rim so the border can be seen.*

• *Balance colors in a salad for interest and appetite appeal.*

• *Ingredients mounded on a plate are more attractive than when spread flat. Arrange fruit wedges or tomato slices in overlapping patterns. Cut ingredients into bite-sized pieces.*

• *Keep it simple. An overly elaborate design or a plate that's too cluttered is not as appealing as an easy, natural arrangement.*

POTATO SALAD WITH FRESH PEAS

Fresh peas enhance a sturdy salad which completes any meal of burgers.

5	potatoes (unpeeled), about 2 lb/1 kg	5
2 tbsp	wine vinegar	25 mL
2 tbsp	vegetable oil	25 mL
1/2 cup	shelled peas	125 mL
1/4 cup	minced fresh parsley	50 mL
1/4 cup	diced celery	50 mL
1/4 cup	chopped green onions	50 mL
1/4 cup	diced sweet red pepper	50 mL
1/3 cup	mayonnaise	75 mL
1/3 cup	sour cream	75 mL
1 tbsp	Dijon mustard	15 mL
1/4 tsp	each salt, pepper and celery seed	1 mL
	Fresh parsley sprigs	

• In large saucepan, cover potatoes with cold salted water, cook just until tender but not mushy. Drain and return potatoes to low heat to dry for a few seconds. Let cool just enough to handle; peel and chop neatly. Place in salad bowl; sprinkle with vinegar and oil, tossing to coat potatoes evenly.

• Meanwhile, in pot of boiling salted water, cook peas just until tender, about 5 minutes. (If using frozen peas, don't cook them; simply run cold water over them.) Drain; refresh under cold running water. Drain again. Add peas, parsley, celery, onions and red pepper to potatoes; toss together gently.

• In small bowl, stir together mayonnaise, sour cream, mustard, salt, pepper and celery seed. Add to potato mixture and mix well. Taste and adjust seasoning. Garnish with parsley sprigs. Makes about 4 servings.

SUPER SLAW

Shred the cabbage finely with a large knife for this good-looking salad. Use regular green cabbage, or use half Chinese cabbage for its pleasant texture and tang. A little red cabbage adds lively color. (photo, p.23)

8 cups	shredded cabbage	2 L
1 cup	chopped onions	250 mL
1 cup	grated carrots	250 mL
1 cup	sliced radishes	250 mL
1/2 cup	vegetable oil	125 mL
1/2 cup	white vinegar	125 mL
1/4 cup	granulated sugar	50 mL
1-1/2 tsp	salt	7 mL
1 tsp	celery seeds	5 mL
1/2 tsp	dry mustard	2 mL
1/4 tsp	pepper	1 mL
1/4 cup	sour cream	50 mL

• In large bowl, combine cabbage, onions, carrots and radishes. In small saucepan, combine oil, vinegar, sugar, salt, celery seeds, mustard and pepper; stir over low heat to dissolve sugar. Remove from heat and add sour cream, whisking until smooth.
• Pour dressing over vegetables and mix well. Slaw can be served immediately or chilled before serving; keeps several days in refrigerator. Makes about 8 servings.

GREEK SALAD

Broccoli and cauliflower add color, flavor and flair to a classic Greek salad. Use Kalamata olives if available for extra flavor. If desired, add chopped lettuce to the salad just before serving, and toss.

1	red onion	1
Half	bunch broccoli	Half
Half	head cauliflower	Half
2	tomatoes	2
1	English cucumber	1
1/2 lb	feta cheese	250 g
2	hard-cooked eggs	2
1/4 cup	black olives	50 mL
DRESSING:		
3/4 cup	olive oil (preferably extra virgin)	175 mL
2 tbsp	red wine vinegar	25 mL
2 tbsp	lemon juice	25 mL
1 tsp	salt	5 mL
1/2 tsp	dried oregano	2 mL
1/4 tsp	pepper	1 mL
1	clove garlic, minced	1

• Peel onion and cut into chunks. Soak in ice water for 30 minutes. Drain and set aside.
• Meanwhile, peel and dice broccoli stalks. Divide broccoli and cauliflower into florets. In large saucepan of boiling water, cook broccoli for about 3 minutes or until tender-crisp. Place in bowl of cold water until chilled; drain and pat dry. Repeat with cauliflower.
• Cut tomatoes, cucumber, feta cheese and eggs into chunks. On large serving plate, arrange onion, broccoli, cauliflower, tomatoes, cucumber, cheese, eggs and olives in rows.
• **Dressing:** In small bowl, combine oil, vinegar, lemon juice, salt, oregano, pepper and garlic. Drizzle over salad. Makes 4 to 6 servings.

COMPOSED SALADS

Make your salads beautiful by arranging the ingredients in attractive layers or patterns. Composed salads usually consist of a base such as lettuce, which provides a background for other artistically arranged food such as meat, cheese, vegetables or pasta. Drizzle a flavorful dressing over your creation and add fresh simple garnishes to complete your work of art.

Chef's Salad; Greek Salad

CHEF'S SALAD

Asparagus is a welcome addition to this chef's salad, but you can substitute green beans if desired. For extra flavor, use double-smoked Black Forest ham.

3	Belgian endives, shredded	3
1	small head Boston lettuce, shredded	1
1	small head red leaf lettuce, shredded	1
1 lb	asparagus, cooked	500 g
1/2 lb	smoked turkey or chicken, julienned	250 g
1/2 lb	rare roast beef, julienned	250 g
1/2 lb	Black Forest ham, julienned	250 g
1/2 lb	Havarti cheese, julienned	250 g
3 tbsp	chopped fresh parsley	50 mL

DRESSING:		
3 tbsp	red wine vinegar	50 mL
1 tsp	Dijon mustard	5 mL
1 tsp	salt	5 mL
1/4 tsp	pepper	1 mL
1/4 tsp	dried oregano (or 1 tsp/5 mL fresh)	1 mL
1/4 tsp	dried thyme (or 1 tsp/5 mL fresh)	1 mL
1/4 tsp	paprika	1 mL
3/4 cup	olive oil	175 mL

• Toss together endives, Boston and leaf lettuce; arrange in salad bowl, mounding in centre. Arrange asparagus, turkey, roast beef, ham and cheese like spokes of wheel over lettuce. Sprinkle with parsley.

• **Dressing:** In small bowl, combine vinegar, mustard, salt, pepper, oregano, thyme and paprika; whisk in oil. Drizzle over salad. Makes 4 to 6 servings.

WHITE BEAN SALAD WITH RED ONION AND PARSLEY

This salad goes well with barbecued pork, hamburgers, sausages and lamb chops.

1	can (19 oz/540 mL) white kidney beans, drained	1
	Half a red onion	
3/4 cup	sliced radishes	175 mL
1	clove garlic, minced	1
1/4 cup	finely chopped fresh parsley	50 mL
2/3 cup	Classic Vinaigrette (recipe, p.113)	150 mL
	Salt and pepper	
	Red leaf lettuce	

• In sieve or colander, rinse beans under cold running water; drain. Thinly slice onion and separate into rings.

• In salad bowl, combine beans, onion, radishes, garlic, parsley and vinaigrette; toss to mix. Season with salt and pepper to taste. (Salad can be prepared to this point and refrigerated for up to 1 day.)

• At serving time, arrange salad on bed of red lettuce. Makes 4 to 6 servings.

White Bean Salad with Red Onion and Parsley; Yogurt Orange Dressing

CLASSIC VINAIGRETTE

Keep this dressing on hand in the refrigerator to use on a variety of salads. Recipe can be doubled.

1/4 cup	white wine vinegar	50 mL
1 tsp	Dijon mustard	5 mL
3/4 tsp	salt	4 mL
	Pepper	
1	clove garlic, minced	1
3/4 cup	vegetable oil	175 mL
1 tbsp	chopped fresh herbs (tarragon, chives, parsley), optional	15 mL

• In bowl, whisk together vinegar, mustard, salt, and pepper to taste; stir in garlic. Gradually whisk in oil. Stir in fresh herbs (if using). Cover and refrigerate for up to 1 week. Makes about 1 cup (250 mL).

SALAD SMARTS

• *Wash and dry greens thoroughly so the dressing will adhere to the leaves and not be diluted. Salad spin-dryers are great for drying greens but paper towels and tea towels work well, too.*
• *If you don't have a large salad bowl, toss the salad in a large pot or mixing bowl, then arrange on platter.*
• *When doubling a salad recipe, you may not need twice as much dressing. Add just enough to moisten salad thoroughly. Pass extra dressing separately.*

THOUSAND ISLAND DRESSING

This dressing is easy to prepare and makes any lettuce salad a sensation.

1/2 cup	plain yogurt	125 mL
1 tbsp	chopped stuffed olives	15 mL
1 tbsp	chili sauce	15 mL
1 tbsp	finely chopped onion	15 mL
1 tbsp	finely chopped sweet green pepper	15 mL
1	hard-cooked egg, chopped	1
	Chopped fresh parsley	

• In bowl, stir together yogurt, olives, chili sauce, onion, green pepper, egg, and parsley to taste; mix well. Transfer to covered container and refrigerate for up to 3 days. Makes about 3/4 cup (175 mL).

YOGURT ORANGE DRESSING

This quick and easy dressing is delicious with fresh fruit.

3/4 cup	plain yogurt	175 mL
1/4 cup	vegetable oil	50 mL
2 tbsp	frozen orange juice concentrate, thawed	25 mL
2 tbsp	liquid honey	25 mL
1/2 tsp	grated orange rind	2 mL

• In small bowl, combine yogurt, oil, orange juice, honey and orange rind; mix thoroughly. Cover and refrigerate for up to 1 day. Makes about 1-1/4 cups (300 mL).

ROMAINE SALAD WITH BLUE CHEESE AND PINE NUTS

Romaine Salad with Blue Cheese and Pine Nuts

Add an extra summery touch to green salads with garnishes of edible flowers. Geraniums, rose petals, violets, chrysanthemums, impatiens, lavender, lilacs, nasturtiums and pansies are just a few suitable blooms.

1	small Spanish onion, sliced in rings	1
1	head romaine lettuce	1
2/3 cup	crumbled blue cheese (about 4 oz/ 125 g)	150 mL
1/4 cup	toasted pine nuts	50 mL
	Creamy Salad Dressing (recipe follows)	

• Soak onion rings in ice water for 15 minutes; drain and pat dry. Arrange lettuce leaves attractively on individual plates. Sprinkle with onion, cheese and pine nuts. Pass Creamy Salad Dressing separately. Makes 4 to 6 servings.

CREAMY SALAD DRESSING:

1	egg yolk	1
3 tbsp	lemon juice	50 mL
1 tsp	Dijon mustard	5 mL
1	small clove garlic, minced	1
2/3 cup	vegetable oil	150 mL
	White pepper	
2 tbsp	toasted pine nuts	25 mL

• In food processor or blender, combine egg yolk, lemon juice, mustard and garlic. With machine running, gradually pour oil in steady stream through feed tube. Season with pepper to taste. Transfer to serving dish; stir in pine nuts. Makes about 3/4 cup (175 mL).

GREEN SALAD SUGGESTIONS

A simple green salad composed of several kinds of interesting lettuces and tossed with a homemade dressing is a light, easy and delicious first course. Allow one small head of Boston lettuce for four servings. For six people, use half a head of Boston lettuce and one small head radicchio (or half a head red leaf lettuce) with a few sprigs of watercress, spinach leaves, romaine lettuce, alfalfa sprouts or Belgian endive.

Choice of salad ingredients depends on your menu and the season. If in doubt, serve a salad of greens, adding one or two extras. Choose as additions:
• vegetables (cooked or raw)—as simple as sliced mushrooms or thinly sliced red onion
• cheese (grated or cubed)
• chopped hard-cooked egg
• meat (crumbled cooked bacon or ham cubes)
• seafood (tuna, salmon, shrimp, crab, mussels, anchovies, sardines)
• fruit (grapes, melon balls, sliced apple, orange wedges)
• croutons

FRENCH DRESSING

Try the interesting variations to this popular tangy dressing.

1/4 cup	(approx) wine vinegar or lemon juice	50 mL
1 tsp	dry mustard	5 mL
1/4 tsp	salt	1 mL
	Pepper	
2/3 cup	(approx) olive, corn or safflower oil or combination	150 mL

• In bowl, whisk together vinegar, mustard, salt, and pepper to taste. Gradually whisk in oil. Taste and add more vinegar or oil, if necessary. Store in covered jar in refrigerator for up to 1 week. Shake well before using. Makes about 1 cup (250 mL).

VARIATIONS:

GARLIC FRENCH DRESSING:
• Add 2 or 3 cloves of minced garlic to French Dressing and marinate in refrigerator for 2 days. Strain before using.

HERBED FRENCH DRESSING:
• Add 1 tbsp (15 mL) fresh herbs or 1/2 tsp (2 mL) dried herbs (tarragon, chives, chervil or parsley) to French Dressing.

BUTTERMILK DRESSING

This creamy dressing goes well with mixed garden greens, chilled cooked fish, seafood or chicken.

2/3 cup	buttermilk	150 mL
1/2 cup	2% cottage cheese	125 mL
2 tbsp	chopped fresh parsley	25 mL
2 tbsp	snipped fresh chives	25 mL
1 tbsp	chopped fresh dill (or 1/4 tsp/1 mL dried dillweed)	15 mL
1/4 tsp	dried tarragon	1 mL
1/4 tsp	salt	1 mL

• In food processor or blender, blend buttermilk with cottage cheese until smooth. Blend in parsley, chives, dill, tarragon and salt. Transfer to covered container and refrigerate until well chilled or for up to 3 days. Makes about 1-1/4 cups (300 mL).

LAYERED SALAD WITH LEMONY FRENCH DRESSING

Substitute other greens for the leaf lettuce and use any of your favorite vegetables in this traditional overnight layered salad.

4 cups	torn leaf lettuce	1 L
1	cucumber, diced	1
2	tomatoes, chopped	2
1/2 cup	sliced green onions	125 mL
1	small red onion, sliced in rings	1
1	stalk celery, sliced	1
1	can (14 oz/398 mL) artichoke hearts, drained	1

LEMONY FRENCH DRESSING:

3 tbsp	lemon juice	50 mL
1 tbsp	white wine vinegar	15 mL
1 tsp	salt	5 mL
1 tsp	granulated sugar	5 mL
1/4 tsp	pepper	1 mL
1/4 tsp	dry mustard	1 mL
3/4 cup	vegetable oil	175 mL

• In large glass salad bowl, layer lettuce, then cucumber, tomatoes, green onions, red onion rings and celery. Top with artichokes.

• **Lemony French Dressing:** Combine lemon juice, vinegar, salt, sugar, pepper and mustard; whisk in oil. Transfer to serving pitcher and pass separately. Makes 6 to 8 servings.

Layered Salad with Lemony French Dressing

PASTA SALAD WITH FETA DRESSING

Dress this robust salad a day ahead, adding tomatoes and cucumber just before serving.

2 cups	pasta shells	500 mL
1 tbsp	olive oil	15 mL
1/3 cup	diced sweet red pepper	75 mL
1/4 cup	chopped green onions	50 mL
1/4 cup	slivered black olives	50 mL
1/4 cup	feta cheese	50 mL
3 tbsp	white wine vinegar	50 mL
2 tbsp	minced fresh parsley	25 mL
1	clove garlic, minced	1
1/2 tsp	dried oregano	2 mL
1/4 tsp	salt	1 mL
1/4 tsp	pepper	1 mL
1/3 cup	olive oil	75 mL
1 cup	halved cherry tomatoes	250 mL
1/2 cup	coarsely chopped seeded cucumber	125 mL
6	tender leaves romaine lettuce	6

• In pot of boiling salted water, cook pasta until al dente (tender but firm), about 8 minutes; drain. Rinse under cold running water; drain again.
• In bowl, combine pasta with 1 tbsp (15 mL) olive oil. Add red pepper, onion and olives.
• In small bowl, mash feta cheese with vinegar; mix in parsley, garlic, oregano, salt and pepper. Whisk in 1/3 cup (75 mL) oil.
• Add tomatoes and cucumbers to pasta; drizzle with dressing and toss lightly to mix. Taste and adjust seasoning.
• Line serving bowl with lettuce; mound with salad. Makes about 4 servings.

Use other pasta shapes for Pasta Salad with Feta Dressing. Choose from farfalle (small bows), penne (like quill pens), elbows, fusilli (long spirals), or rotini (short spirals). Colored pasta—spinach, basil, tomato or whole wheat—makes a pleasant change as well.

Remember to cook until al dente (tender but firm); drain and rinse under cold water and drain again.

CHILLED GREEN PEA SALAD WITH DILL

Fresh peas are wonderful in this salad, but you can use tender young frozen peas if you wish. Make this several hours in advance, if desired. (photo, p.18)

2 cups	shelled fresh green peas	500 mL
1 cup	plain yogurt	250 mL
1 tbsp	chopped fresh dill	15 mL
2 tsp	lemon juice	10 mL
1 tsp	chopped fresh chives	5 mL
1/2 tsp	curry powder	2 mL
	Salt and pepper	
GARNISH:		
1/4 cup	chopped pimiento	50 mL
	Red pepper rings and dill sprigs (optional)	

• In pot of boiling water, cook peas for about 3 minutes or just until almost tender; drain well.
• Meanwhile, in small serving bowl, combine yogurt, dill, lemon juice, chives, curry powder, and salt and pepper to taste; stir in peas. Cover and refrigerate.
• **Garnish:** Serve with pimiento, and red pepper and dill (if using). Makes 8 to 10 servings.

GRILLED MARINATED MUSHROOMS

For colorful vegetable kabobs, try marinating other partially cooked vegetables, such as carrots, broccoli, cauliflower or brussels sprouts.

1 lb	large mushrooms	500 g
MARINADE:		
3/4 cup	vegetable oil	175 mL
1/4 cup	cider vinegar	50 mL
1	clove garlic, minced	1
1 tsp	granulated sugar	5 mL
1 tsp	celery seeds	5 mL
1/2 tsp	dry mustard	2 mL
1/2 tsp	salt	2 mL
1/4 tsp	pepper	1 mL

- Remove stems from mushrooms; reserve for another use.
- **Marinade:** In large bowl, mix together oil, vinegar, garlic, sugar, celery seeds, mustard, salt and pepper. Add mushroom caps and toss gently. Cover and refrigerate for 2 hours.
- Drain caps, reserving marinade. Thread onto greased metal or soaked wooden skewers, hollow side up. Cook on greased grill over medium-hot coals or on medium setting for 5 to 7 minutes or until tender, basting occasionally with reserved marinade. Do not turn. Makes 4 servings.

BARBECUED BEANS

This updated, lighter version of old-fashioned beans can be finished right on the barbecue. (photo, p.54)

10 oz	dried pinto beans	280 g
6 cups	cold water	1.5 L
1/4 tsp	salt	1 mL
2 tbsp	vegetable oil	25 mL
1/4 lb	smoked cooked ham, diced	125 g
1	onion, coarsely chopped	1
1	stalk celery, coarsely chopped	1
1	clove garlic, minced	1
Half	large sweet green pepper, cubed	Half
Half	can (5-1/2 oz/156 mL) tomato paste	Half
1/4 cup	chili sauce	50 mL
1 tbsp	packed brown sugar	15 mL
1-1/2 tsp	dry mustard	7 mL
1-1/2 tsp	white vinegar	7 mL
1/2 tsp	salt	2 mL
1/4 tsp	pepper	1 mL

- Rinse beans, discarding any shrivelled or discolored ones. In large pot, bring beans and cold water to boil; reduce heat and simmer, uncovered, for 2 minutes. Remove from heat; cover and let stand for 1 hour. (Alternatively, soak beans in cold water overnight.)
- Do not drain. Add 1/4 tsp (1 mL) salt and bring to boil; reduce heat and simmer, covered, for 1-1/2 to 2 hours or until beans begin to soften. Tip pot to drain beans, reserving 2 cups (500 mL) of the liquid.
- Return 1-1/2 cups (375 mL) of the liquid to pot, reserving remaining liquid; return pot to heat.
- Meanwhile, in large skillet or medium saucepan, heat oil over medium-high heat; cook ham, onion, celery, garlic and green pepper for 5 minutes or until vegetables are softened. Stir in tomato paste, chili sauce, brown sugar, mustard, vinegar, salt and pepper. Bring to boil; reduce heat and simmer, uncovered, for 15 minutes. Add mixture to beans.
- Place pot on barbecue grill and simmer, uncovered, for 30 to 45 minutes or until beans and vegetables are tender, adding some of the reserved cooking liquid if beans become dry. Taste and adjust seasoning if necessary. Makes 8 to 10 servings.

HERBED BUTTER FOR CORN-ON-THE-COB

The flavor of fresh herbs complements tender corn-on-the-cob. In small bowl, whip 1 cup (250 mL) butter with fork. Blend in 1 tbsp (15 mL) finely chopped parsley, 1 tbsp (15 mL) snipped fresh chives, pinch chopped fresh thyme, dash lemon juice, and pepper to taste. On waxed paper, shape into log. Wrap in plastic and refrigerate until chilled. Makes about 1 cup (250 mL).

For a fast, sweet and delectable treat, grill corn-on-the-cob. Peel back the husks, remove silk and rewrap the husks. Soak corn in cold water for 1 hour. Place directly on coals and cook, turning frequently, for about 15 minutes or until corn is tender.

Corn-on-the-Cob

CRISP POTATO ROSES

These elegant roses are composed of very thinly sliced potatoes arranged petal-like in custard cups. Use small potatoes, all about the same size. (photo, p.17)

3/4 cup	unsalted butter	175 mL
1	clove garlic, halved	1
1 tsp	each dried thyme and salt	5 mL
1/4 tsp	each pepper and dried rosemary	1 mL
3 lb	small potatoes (unpeeled)	1.5 kg

• In small saucepan, melt butter with garlic over low heat. Skim off any white solids and discard garlic. Brush eight 3/4-cup (175 mL) custard cups or individual quiche pans with some of the butter. Stir thyme, salt, pepper and rosemary into remaining butter; set aside.
• Peel potatoes; place in bowl of cold water. Drain and dry each potato as needed. With vegetable peeler or thin slicing blade of food processor, slice potatoes as thinly as possible. As you work, add slices from each potato to butter mixture, tossing well to coat. Using slotted spoon, transfer slices in batches to large bowl.
• Starting at outer edge of each prepared custard cup, overlap potato slices in circle. Arrange second overlapping circle on top about 1 inch (2.5 cm) below top edge. Continue circles into centre. Dot with any remaining butter. (Potatoes can be prepared ahead to this point and stand at room temperature for up to 1 hour.)
• Bake in 450°F (230°C) oven for 30 to 40 minutes or until potatoes are golden brown, crisp and tender when pierced in centre with fork. Makes 8 servings.

Herbed Vegetable
Casserole

HERBED VEGETABLE CASSEROLE

*Here's a delicious dish that features tender
summer vegetables.*

1/4 cup	butter	50 mL
4	new potatoes (unpeeled), cut in 1/4-inch (5 mm) slices	4
1 tbsp	each finely chopped fresh sage and tarragon (or 1 tsp/5 mL each dried)	15 mL
	Salt	
3	sweet red or green peppers, cut in 1/4-inch (5 mm) dice	3
1	onion, thinly sliced	1
1/2 cup	long-grain rice	125 mL
3	zucchini (each about 6 in/15 cm long), thinly sliced	3
4	tomatoes, thickly sliced	4
1 cup	shredded Swiss cheese (about 4 oz/ 125 g)	250 mL
	Sage sprigs (optional)	

• Using some of the butter, grease 10-cup
(2.5 L) baking dish. Arrange half the potato
slices in overlapping rows in dish. Dot with a
little of the butter and sprinkle with pinch of
sage, tarragon, and salt to taste; layer with
half the red peppers, half the onion, half the
rice and half the zucchini. Dot with butter;
sprinkle with sage, tarragon, and salt to taste.
Repeat layers. Arrange tomatoes over top.

• Cover with foil and bake in 350°F (180°C)
oven for 1-1/2 to 1-3/4 hours or until potatoes
are tender. Sprinkle with cheese; cover and
bake for about 10 minutes longer or until
cheese is melted. Let stand, covered, for 10
minutes before serving. Garnish with sage
sprigs (if using). Makes 6 to 8 servings.

GRILLED ONION SALAD

Grilling lends onions a special flavor that's made even more interesting with the addition of a slightly sweet vinaigrette. For best results, partially cover the barbecue with a lid. (photo, p.17)

(photo, p.17)

4	medium red onions (unpeeled)	4
1/4 cup	olive oil	50 mL
2 tbsp	lemon juice	25 mL
2 tbsp	white wine vinegar	25 mL
Pinch	cayenne pepper	Pinch
1 tbsp	granulated sugar	15 mL
1/2 tsp	salt	2 mL
1/4 tsp	black pepper	1 mL
	Chopped fresh parsley (optional)	

- Peel onions, leaving stem ends intact. Cut shallow cross in root ends.
- In large bowl, stir together oil, lemon juice, vinegar and cayenne. Add onions, rolling to coat well. Let stand for 30 minutes, rolling onions in mixture occasionally.
- With slotted spoon, remove onions; stir sugar, salt and black pepper into marinade and set aside.
- Cook onions on greased grill over medium-hot coals or on medium setting, turning every 5 minutes, for about 30 minutes or just until lightly charred all over and tender when pierced with knife. Let cool slightly; remove stems and charred outer layers.
- In food processor fitted with thin slicing blade or using very sharp knife, cut onions into very thin slices. Toss with reserved marinade. Cover and refrigerate for at least 4 hours or overnight. Just before serving, arrange onions on individual salad plates. Garnish with parsley (if using). Makes 8 servings.

NEW POTATO SALAD WITH CELERY

Moist, waxy new potatoes are ideal for salads. This recipe makes enough for a party. Halve the recipe for fewer servings. (photo, p.12)

(photo, p.12)

6 lb	waxy new potatoes, unpeeled (about 14 large)	2.75 kg
1/2 cup	white wine vinegar	125 mL
1/4 cup	dry white wine or chicken stock	50 mL
1/3 cup	vegetable oil	75 mL
1 cup	coarsely chopped onions	250 mL
8	tender stalks celery	8
2 cups	mayonnaise	500 mL
1/2 cup	finely chopped fresh parsley	125 mL
1/4 cup	sour cream	50 mL
3 tbsp	Dijon mustard	50 mL
2 tbsp	chopped fresh dill (or 2 tsp/10 mL dried dillweed)	25 mL
2 tsp	salt	10 mL
1 tsp	pepper	5 mL

- In large saucepan, cover potatoes with cold salted water; cook just until tender but not mushy. Drain and return potatoes to low heat, cook, uncovered, for 1 to 2 minutes to dry potatoes. Let cool just enough to handle; peel and cut into 3/4-inch (2 cm) cubes. Transfer to large bowl; drizzle with vinegar and wine. Toss together gently.
- In large skillet, heat oil over medium-high heat; sauté onions for 5 to 8 minutes or until tender but not browned. Add to potatoes and toss gently; let cool to room temperature.
- Trim leaves from celery; reserve for garnish. Cut celery stalks diagonally into slices; add to potatoes.
- In separate bowl, combine mayonnaise, parsley, sour cream, mustard, dill, salt and pepper; mix into salad. Cover and refrigerate for 1 to 2 hours. Taste and adjust seasoning, if necessary. Spoon into large salad bowl; garnish with reserved celery leaves. Makes 20 servings.

VEGETABLES ON THE BARBECUE

To simplify barbecued meals and to cut down on cooking time, you can barbecue vegetables alongside the main course.

- *To steam vegetables on the barbecue: Slice, dice or julienne large vegetables; small vegetables can be grilled whole. Place vegetables on large greased pieces of foil, sprinkle with herbs, minced garlic, olive oil, butter, soy sauce or grated cheese. Fold up foil to form sealed packets.*
- *Vegetables such as carrots, beans, onions and potatoes take longer to cook than vegetables such as mushrooms, tomatoes and zucchini and should be placed in separate sealed packets.*

VEGETABLE KABOBS

If crookneck squash is unavailable, substitute butternut squash or more zucchini. (photo, p.75)

2	yellow crookneck squash	2
2	zucchini	2
16	small white onions	16
2	large fennel (anise) bulbs	2
2	large sweet green peppers	2
MARINADE:		
3/4 cup	vegetable oil	175 mL
1/4 cup	lemon juice	50 mL
2 tbsp	minced fresh basil (or 1 tbsp/15 mL dried)	25 mL
2 tbsp	minced fresh parsley	25 mL
2 tbsp	red wine vinegar	25 mL
1 tbsp	Dijon mustard	15 mL
1	bay leaf	1
1/2 tsp	dried thyme	2 mL
1/2 tsp	dried marjoram	2 mL
2	cloves garlic, minced	2

• In pot of boiling water, blanch squash and zucchini for 5 minutes; drain well. Peel squash; cut each squash and zucchini into 8 chunks and place in large bowl.

• In pot of boiling water, blanch onions and fennel bulbs for 7 minutes; drain and peel. Leave onions whole but cut fennel into 1/2-inch (1 cm) thick slices; add to bowl. Cut green peppers into eighths and discard seeds; add to bowl.

• **Marinade:** Combine oil, lemon juice, basil, parsley, vinegar, mustard, bay leaf, thyme, marjoram and garlic; mix well. Pour over vegetables and toss gently. Cover and marinate in refrigerator for at least 2 hours or overnight.

• Drain vegetables, reserving marinade for basting. Thread vegetables alternately onto greased skewers. Cook over medium-hot coals or on medium setting, turning and basting with marinade frequently, for about 15 minutes or until vegetables are tender. Makes 6 to 8 servings.

You can mix and match any of the following vegetables for kabobs:

• Parboiled—baby beets, small new potatoes, brussels sprouts, sliced carrots, 2-inch (2.5 cm) chunks of corn-on-the-cob, sweet potato chunks, baby artichokes.
• Blanched—broccoli florets, asparagus, green bean bundles tied with green onions.
• Uncooked—cherry tomatoes, mushrooms, green or red bell pepper cubes.

Brush vegetables with oil or a marinade before cooking over medium-hot coals or on medium setting; cook until lightly browned and fork-tender.

RATATOUILLE

This is an easy way to prepare this classic vegetable combination. (photo, p.46)

1	small eggplant	1
3	tomatoes	3
2	zucchini	2
1	large onion, coarsely chopped	1
1	sweet green pepper, seeded and cut in thin strips	1
1	clove garlic, finely chopped	1
1/4 cup	vegetable oil	50 mL
1 tsp	salt	5 mL
1/2 tsp	granulated sugar	2 mL
1/2 tsp	dried thyme	2 mL
Pinch	pepper	Pinch
	Chopped fresh parsley	

• Peel and quarter eggplant; cut into 1/8-inch (3 mm) thick slices. Cut tomatoes into quarters. Cut zucchini into 1/8-inch (3 mm) thick slices.

• In bowl, combine eggplant, tomatoes, zucchini, onion, green pepper, garlic, oil, salt, sugar, thyme and pepper; toss until well mixed.

• Cut six 16-inch (40 cm) squares of heavy-duty foil. Divide vegetable mixture evenly and place on foil. Fold foil to make packets, using double fold and leaving space for expansion; seal ends.

• Cook packets on greased grill over medium-hot coals or on medium setting, turning once, for 30 minutes or until zucchini is tender. Cut "X" in top of package and roll back corners. Sprinkle with parsley. Serve in packages or remove to serving dish. Makes 6 servings.

ASPARAGUS MOUSSE

For a delightful change, try a creamy, light vegetable mousse. Garnish with herb sprigs, asparagus spears, tomato roses, cucumber twists, red pepper slices, black olives or fresh flowers.

2 lb	asparagus	1 kg
1/2 cup	mayonnaise	125 mL
4 tsp	lemon juice	20 mL
1 tbsp	chopped green onion	15 mL
2	envelopes unflavored gelatin	2
1/2 cup	water	125 mL
1 cup	whipping cream	250 mL
2	egg whites	2
1 tsp	salt	5 mL

Asparagus Mousse

- Break off tough stems from asparagus and discard. Peel asparagus stems; cut into 1-inch (2.5 cm) lengths. In saucepan of boiling salted water, cook asparagus for about 10 minutes or until tender; drain. In food processor or blender, process until smooth. There should be about 2 cups (500 mL) purée. Transfer to saucepan. Add mayonnaise, lemon juice and onion; cook over low heat, stirring, just until warmed through.
- Meanwhile, in small saucepan, sprinkle gelatin over water; let stand for 5 minutes to soften.
- Over low heat, warm gelatin until dissolved; stir into asparagus mixture. Transfer to bowl and place in large bowl of ice and water to chill, stirring frequently, for 10 to 15 minutes or until cold and slightly thickened. Remove from ice water.
- Whip cream; set aside. In large bowl, beat egg whites with salt until stiff peaks form. Whisk about one-quarter of the beaten egg whites into cooled asparagus mixture; fold into remaining whites along with whipped cream. Pour into rinsed but not dried 6-cup (1.5 L) mould. Cover and refrigerate for at least 6 hours or up to 2 days.
- To unmould, wrap hot damp tea towel around mould for 1 minute. Using knife, loosen top edge of mousse from mould. Tilt or gently shake mould to loosen mousse. Invert rinsed serving platter on top of mould. Grasp platter and mould; quickly turn over. Shake, using quick downward motion, to release mousse from mould. Lift off mould. (If mousse sticks, repeat procedure.) Makes 4 to 6 servings.

VARIATIONS:

TOMATO BASIL:
- Substitute 3 large tomatoes (1-1/2 lb/750 g) for the asparagus. Omit lemon juice and add 1/2 cup (125 mL) chopped fresh basil (or 1/2 cup/125 mL chopped fresh parsley and 2 tsp/ 10 mL dried basil). To prepare tomatoes: Peel, seed and coarsely chop. In food processor or blender, process until smooth. There should be about 2 cups (500 mL). Complete mousse as directed above.

CUCUMBER MINT:
- Substitute 3 cucumbers (2 lb/1 kg) for the asparagus and add 1/2 cup (125 mL) chopped fresh mint. To prepare cucumbers: Peel, seed and coarsely chop. In food processor or blender, process until smooth. There should be about 2 cups (500 mL). Complete mousse as directed above.

RED PEPPER:
- Substitute 4 large sweet red peppers (2 lb/ 1 kg) for the asparagus. Omit green onion and add 2 cloves garlic (minced), pinch dried thyme and dash hot pepper sauce. To prepare peppers: On baking sheet, broil whole peppers, turning several times, for 20 to 25 minutes or until skin is blackened and blistered. Cover with tea towel and let stand for 10 minutes. Peel and halve peppers; discard seeds and membranes and chop coarsely. In food processor or blender, process until smooth. There should be about 2 cups (500 mL). Complete mousse as directed above.

POTATOES DELUXE

When the barbecue's on for grilling, take advantage of the convenience and cook potatoes at the same time. (photo, p.85)

6	baking potatoes	6
	Salt and pepper	
1	small Spanish onion, cut in 6 wedges	1
1	sweet green pepper, cut in strips	1
2 tbsp	butter	25 mL
6	strips bacon	6

• Scrub potatoes; cut V-shaped wedge lengthwise out of top of each one. Sprinkle cut sides with salt and pepper. Insert onion wedge in each; top with green pepper and 1 tsp (5 mL) butter. Wrap bacon around each potato. Place on square of foil and wrap foil tightly around potato.

• Cover and bake on grill over medium-hot coals or on medium setting, turning occasionally, for 35 to 40 minutes or until potatoes are fork-tender. Fold back foil; return potatoes to barbecue. Cover and cook for 5 to 10 minutes longer to crisp bacon. Makes 6 servings.

STIR-FRIED GREEN BEANS WITH RED AND YELLOW PEPPER STRIPS

Cook this colorful, quick side dish while the main course is grilling.

1 lb	green beans, trimmed	500 g
1/4 cup	cold water	50 mL
1 tbsp	soy sauce	15 mL
1 tsp	cornstarch	5 mL
1 tbsp	peanut or vegetable oil	15 mL
Half	each sweet red and yellow pepper, cut in strips	Half
1	clove garlic, minced	1

• In large saucepan of boiling water, cook beans for 3 minutes. Drain and refresh under cold running water. Pat dry. Stir together cold water, soy sauce and cornstarch; set aside.

• In wok or large skillet, heat oil over high heat; stir-fry beans, red and yellow peppers and garlic for 2 to 3 minutes or until beans are tender. Stir cornstarch mixture and add to wok; cook, stirring, for 1 minute. Serve immediately. Makes about 4 servings.

GREEN BEANS WITH TOASTED PINE NUTS

These make-ahead beans can be cooked early in the day, then reheated in butter enhanced with the rich flavor of pine nuts. (photo, p.17)

2 lb	green beans, trimmed	1 kg
1/4 cup	unsalted butter	50 mL
1/2 cup	pine nuts	125 mL
	Salt and pepper	
1 tsp	lemon juice	5 mL

• In large saucepan of boiling salted water, cook beans, uncovered, over medium-high heat for 4 to 5 minutes or just until tender-crisp and still bright green. Immediately drain and refresh under cold running water. Drain well again. (Beans can be prepared ahead to this point, wrapped in clean tea towel and refrigerated for up to 6 hours.)

• In large skillet, melt butter over medium-low heat; cook pine nuts, stirring constantly, for about 4 minutes or until light brown. With slotted spoon, remove to small bowl; set aside.

• Add beans to skillet; shake pan to coat with butter. Season with salt and pepper to taste. Cover and cook for 2 minutes or until heated through. Stir in lemon juice. Arrange in warm shallow serving dish and sprinkle with pine nuts. Makes 8 servings.

NEW POTATOES IN GARLIC-BASIL BUTTER

New potatoes bathed in herbed garlic butter cook to perfection on the barbecue.

For each serving: Scrub 3 or 4 small new potatoes. If using larger potatoes, cut in halves or quarters; peel if desired. Place each serving on square of double-thickness heavy-duty foil. Dot liberally with Garlic-Basil Butter; sprinkle with salt and pepper to taste. Wrap securely in foil. Roast directly on hot coals for about 45 minutes, or on grill just above coals or on high setting for about 1 hour or until tender, turning occasionally.

Garlic-Basil Butter: For about 8 servings, combine 1/2 cup (125 mL) soft butter, 2 cloves finely minced garlic, 2 tbsp (25 mL) each finely minced fresh parsley, chives or green onions and fresh basil (or 2 tsp/ 10 mL dried basil).

Zucchini "Pasta" with Fresh Tomato Sauce

ZUCCHINI "PASTA" WITH FRESH TOMATO SAUCE

Long wide strips of zucchini resemble broad pasta and are easy to make with a vegetable slicer, the slicing side of a grater or a vegetable peeler. The sauced "pasta" makes a light luncheon dish when served with crusty bread or a simple first course for a dinner party.

3 tbsp	olive oil	50 mL
4	large ripe tomatoes, peeled, seeded and chopped	4
2	sprigs fresh thyme (or 1/2 tsp/2 mL dried)	2
1	bay leaf	1
1/2 tsp	granulated sugar	2 mL
1/2 tsp	salt	2 mL
1/4 tsp	pepper	1 mL
6	small zucchini, trimmed (about 1-1/2 lb/750 g)	6
2	cloves garlic, minced	2
	Cayenne pepper	
1 tbsp	freshly grated Parmesan cheese	15 mL

• In saucepan, heat 1 tbsp (15 mL) of the oil over medium heat. Add tomatoes, thyme, bay leaf, sugar, salt and pepper; cook, uncovered, for 7 to 10 minutes or until excess moisture has evaporated. Remove bay leaf.

• Meanwhile, slice unpeeled zucchini lengthwise into long wide strips about 1/8 inch (3 mm) thick. In large skillet, heat 1 tbsp (15 mL) of the remaining oil over high heat. Add half of the zucchini strips and half of the garlic; sprinkle with pinch of cayenne; cook, stirring almost constantly, for about 3 minutes or until zucchini is tender and golden. Remove to paper towel-lined baking sheet and keep warm in low oven. Repeat with remaining oil, zucchini, garlic and cayenne.

• Arrange zucchini mixture on warmed serving platter. Pour sauce over and sprinkle with Parmesan. Serve immediately. Makes about 4 servings.

Desserts

The perfect summer desserts are cool, light and feature the best of the season's fruit and berries. In this section, we offer everything from a simple sauce for fresh fruit to spectacular make-ahead fruit desserts such as Blueberry and Strawberry Tart (p.128) and frozen treats like Frozen Strawberry Mousse with Strawberry Sauce (p.145). Light cakes such as Kiwi Torte (p.137) are perfect for hot-weather dining and you'll even find simple directions for grilling fruit.

STRAWBERRY TART

Combine fresh berries and a luscious cream cheese filling in a tasty pastry for an all-time favorite summer dessert.

PASTRY:

2 cups	all-purpose flour	500 mL
1/2 cup	fruit/berry sugar	125 mL
1 cup	butter, softened	250 mL

FILLING:

Half	envelope (7 g) unflavored gelatin	Half
2 tbsp	lemon juice	25 mL
1 tbsp	boiling water	15 mL
1/4 lb	cream cheese, softened	125 g
1/4 cup	icing sugar	50 mL
1/2 tsp	vanilla	2 mL
1/2 cup	whipping cream	125 mL
4 cups	strawberries, hulled and halved	1 L
1/4 cup	red currant jelly, melted	50 mL

• **Pastry:** In bowl, stir together flour and sugar. With pastry blender or two knives, cut in butter until mixture forms crumbly dough. Press firmly onto bottom and sides of 2 shallow 10- x 4-3/4-inch (25 x 11 cm) foil pans, crimping edges, or onto bottom of 10-inch (3 L) springform pan. Refrigerate for 15 minutes. Bake in 350°F (180°C) oven for 25 to 30 minutes or until lightly golden.
• **Filling:** Sprinkle gelatin over lemon juice; let stand for 1 minute or until softened. Stir in boiling water until gelatin dissolves.
• In large bowl, beat together cream cheese, sugar and vanilla until smooth. Beat in dissolved gelatin. Whip cream; fold into cream cheese mixture. Spoon evenly over each cooled crust; cover and refrigerate for about 1 hour or until set.
• Arrange strawberries over filling; brush strawberries with melted jelly to glaze. Let stand until glaze is set. Makes about 8 servings.

Strawberry Tart

Blueberry and Strawberry Tart

BLUEBERRY AND STRAWBERRY TART

Berry season calls for at least one special pie. This one combines fresh berries, luscious lemon-sour cream filling, and a pastry that handles well and doesn't shrink when baked. For the photograph, some of the strawberries were sliced and fanned out.

HOT WATER PASTRY:

2-1/2 cups	all-purpose flour	625 mL
1/2 tsp	salt	2 mL
3/4 cup	boiling water	175 mL
6 tbsp	shortening, melted	100 mL
2	egg yolks	2
2 tbsp	milk	25 mL

FILLING:

1/2 lb	cream cheese	250 g
2 tbsp	sour cream or plain yogurt	25 mL
1 tbsp	granulated sugar	15 mL
1 tsp	grated lemon rind	5 mL
1 tbsp	lemon juice	15 mL

TOPPING:

4 cups	strawberries	1 L
1 cup	blueberries	250 mL
2 tbsp	apple or currant jelly, melted	25 mL

• **Hot Water Pastry:** In large bowl, stir together flour and salt. Combine water and shortening; pour over flour mixture and mix well with fork. Blend in 1 of the egg yolks; form into ball. On floured surface, knead dough gently; cover with plastic wrap and let stand at room temperature for 30 minutes.
• Roll out two-thirds of the dough into 16- x 12-inch (40 x 30 cm) rectangle. Gently place in 12- x 8-inch (1.5 L) flan pan. Trim pastry, leaving 1-inch (2.5 cm) overhang; fold under, making lip to hold braid.
• Roll out remaining dough into 4-inch (10 cm) square; cut into 9 equal strips. With hands, roll out each strip into 20-inch (50 cm) rope. Braid 3 of the ropes together; repeat with remaining ropes. Dampen edges of pie shell with cold water; gently press braids onto edges.
• With fork, prick bottom and sides of pastry; line with foil and weigh down with pie weights. Combine milk and remaining egg yolk; brush over braids. Bake in 425°F (220°C) oven for 10 minutes. Remove foil and weights; bake for 5 to 8 minutes longer or until golden. Remove sides of pan and let cool.
• **Filling:** In food processor or bowl, combine cream cheese, sour cream, sugar, lemon rind and juice until well mixed and spreadable; spread over pastry.
• **Topping:** Arrange alternating rows of strawberries and blueberries over filling. Using pastry brush, glaze with jelly. Refrigerate for up to 3 hours. Makes 8 to 10 servings.

FRUIT KABOBS

Fruit kabobs are delicious when simply warmed over the grill and served with a rich dipping sauce.

Select a variety of fruits and cut into slices or chunks. Try whole strawberries, large grapes, chunks of kiwifruit, banana, pineapple, melon, apples, pears and peaches.

Thread fruit chunks onto skewers; brush with melted butter and sprinkle lightly with sugar. Cook quickly on grill, turning often until glazed and warm. Don't overcook. Serve immediately with warm chocolate fondue from the recipe for Strawberry Shortcake Kabobs, p. 129. Keep fondue warm on edge of barbecue, watching that chocolate doesn't scorch.

Strawberry Shortcake Kabob

STRAWBERRY SHORTCAKE KABOBS

This is an imaginative alternative to traditional strawberry shortcake. Serve these strawberry and pound cake kabobs drizzled with chocolate sauce and a dab of whipped cream. Or, double the chocolate sauce recipe, and transfer it to a fondue pot to keep warm while enjoying a summery chocolate fondue.

9	slices (each 1/2 inch/1 cm thick) pound cake	9
24	strawberries, hulled (approx 2-1/2 cups/625 mL)	24
4 oz	semisweet chocolate	125 g
2 tbsp	butter	25 mL
1 tbsp	mint or orange liqueur (optional)	15 mL
1/2 cup	whipping cream	125 mL

• Using 1-inch (2.5 cm) cookie cutter, cut out 18 shapes (hearts, diamonds, stars, circles or squares) from slices of pound cake. Alternately thread strawberries and pound cake onto 6 skewers. Set aside.

• In top of double boiler over hot not boiling water, melt chocolate with butter, stirring until smooth. (Alternatively, in microwaveable dish, microwave at Medium/50% for 1 to 2 minutes or until melted; stir until smooth.) Stir in liqueur (if using). Drizzle sauce over kabobs. Whip cream and pass separately. Makes 6 servings.

STRAWBERRY-RHUBARB FLAN

Make this dessert a day ahead. The pastry stays crisp and delicious.

ALMOND PASTRY CRUST:

1/2 cup	butter, softened	125 mL
1/3 cup	ground almonds	75 mL
1/4 cup	granulated sugar	50 mL
1/4 tsp	salt	1 mL
1/4 tsp	almond extract	1 mL
1 cup	all-purpose flour	250 mL

CUSTARD:

3	egg yolks	3
1/3 cup	granulated sugar	75 mL
2 tbsp	all-purpose flour	25 mL
1/4 tsp	salt	1 mL
1 cup	milk or light cream, scalded	250 mL
1 tbsp	butter	15 mL
1 tsp	vanilla	5 mL

RHUBARB PURÉE:

2 cups	diced rhubarb	500 mL
3/4 cup	granulated sugar	175 mL

STRAWBERRY GLAZE:

3/4 cup	strawberry jelly	175 mL
1/4 cup	water	50 mL
1 tbsp	cornstarch	15 mL
4 cups	strawberries, hulled	1 L

• **Almond Pastry Crust:** In small mixing bowl or in food processor, cream butter until light and fluffy. Blend in almonds, sugar, salt and almond extract. Work in flour until soft dough forms. Wrap dough in plastic wrap or waxed paper and refrigerate until firm enough to roll, about 30 minutes.

• Roll out dough between 2 sheets of waxed paper into 10-inch (25 cm) circle. Ease into 9-inch (23 cm) round flan pan with removable base. Press pastry against side and bottom of pan; prick well with fork. Freeze for 20 minutes.

• Bake pastry in 400°F (200°C) oven for 20 minutes or until golden brown. Let cool completely on wire rack before filling.

• **Custard:** In small saucepan, beat together egg yolks and sugar. Stir in flour and salt. Beating constantly, gradually add hot milk. Bring to boil; reduce heat and cook for 2 minutes, stirring, until custard is thick and smooth. Remove from heat; blend in butter and vanilla. Place plastic wrap or waxed paper directly on custard and refrigerate until cold.

• **Rhubarb Purée:** In saucepan, combine rhubarb with sugar. Bring to boil, stirring to dissolve sugar. Reduce heat; simmer, uncovered, until rhubarb is tender and mixture has thickened, about 20 minutes. Remove from heat and set aside.

• **Strawberry Glaze:** In small saucepan, combine jelly, water and cornstarch. Whisking constantly, bring to boil; cook until thickened.

• Spoon custard into pastry shell and cover with rhubarb purée. Top with whole strawberries, placing largest berry in centre and surrounding with remaining berries in circular pattern. Drizzle with warm strawberry glaze. Refrigerate for several hours, preferably overnight. Makes 8 servings.

FRUIT-FILLED PINEAPPLE WITH RASPBERRY SAUCE

Present a mixture of seasonal fresh fruit in a pineapple shell with a chilled berry sauce. Substitute fresh or frozen strawberries for a flavor change.

1	pineapple	1
	Fresh fruit (berries, melon balls, chopped peaches, chopped pears, etc.)	

RASPBERRY SAUCE:

1	pkg (300 g) frozen sweetened raspberries	1

• Cut off top third of pineapple. Hollow out pineapple, leaving sturdy shell intact; set aside.

• Remove core from cut-out pineapple. Chop pineapple into bite-sized chunks and combine with fresh fruit. Spoon into pineapple shell.

• **Raspberry Sauce:** Thaw raspberries. (Alternatively, combine 2 cups/500 mL fresh raspberries with 1/3 cup/75 mL fruit/berry sugar or more to taste; let stand at room temperature for at least 1 hour.) Press through sieve to remove seeds; chill. Pass separately to pour over individual servings. Makes 4 servings.

Mint Iced Tea (p. 45); Strawberry-Rhubarb Flan

RASPBERRY AND RED CURRANT TARTS

No one will be able to resist the summer flavor of this sweet jamlike filling in tender flaky pastry. Top each tart with whipped cream, if desired, and serve them with forks.

PASTRY:

3 cups	all-purpose flour	750 mL
1 tsp	salt	5 mL
1/2 cup	cold butter, cubed	125 mL
1/2 cup	cold lard, cubed	125 mL
1	egg	1
2 tsp	white vinegar	10 mL
	Ice water	

FILLING:

1/2 cup	water	125 mL
3 tbsp	cornstarch	45 mL
1 cup	granulated sugar	250 mL
1 cup	raspberries	250 mL
1 cup	red currants	250 mL

• **Pastry:** In food processor fitted with metal blade, combine flour and salt; process to mix. Using on/off motion, cut in butter and lard until mixture resembles fine crumbs with a few larger pieces.

• In measuring cup, beat egg until foamy; add vinegar and enough ice water to make 2/3 cup (150 mL).

• With motor running, add egg mixture all at once; process just until dough starts to clump together and form ball. Remove and wrap; chill for at least 30 minutes or for up to 3 days, or freeze for up to 3 months. Let cold pastry stand for 15 minutes at room temperature before rolling out.

• **Filling:** Meanwhile, in small saucepan, stir together water and cornstarch until smooth; stir in sugar. Add raspberries and red currants; bring to simmer, stirring. Reduce heat to medium-low and cook, stirring, for 10 to 15 minutes or until thickened. Remove from heat and let cool.

• Meanwhile, roll out pastry to 1/8-inch (3 mm) thickness. Using 4-inch (10 cm) round cutter, cut out pastry and fit into 3-inch (8 cm) tart tins; place on baking sheet.

• Line each shell with foil and pie weights; bake in 425°F (220°C) oven for 10 minutes. Reduce heat to 350°F (180°C) and bake for 10 minutes longer. Remove weights and foil; bake for 5 minutes longer or until pastry is golden brown.

• Let cool in tins for 15 minutes; gently remove pastry shells to wire rack. Spoon about 4 tsp (20 mL) cooled filling into each shell. Makes about 24 tarts.

FRUIT-FILLED WATERMELON WITH LEMON-LIME SYRUP

Summer-fresh fruit bathed in a refreshing syrup and piled in a decorative container makes both a spectacular and tasty dessert.

1	watermelon	1
18 cups	berries, pineapple chunks, chopped peaches and pears, red and green apples, grapes	4.5 L
1/4 cup	fruit liqueur (melon, orange, peach, pear), optional	50 mL
LEMON-LIME SYRUP:		
1 cup	granulated sugar	250 mL
1/3 cup	water	75 mL
1-1/2 tsp	each grated lemon and lime rind	7 mL
1/3 cup	lemon juice	75 mL
1/4 cup	lime juice	50 mL

- **Lemon-Lime Syrup:** In small saucepan, combine sugar, water, lemon and lime rinds and juices; bring to boil, stirring until sugar dissolves. Remove from heat and let cool.
- Cut out watermelon to make scalloped basket; set aside. Cut out flesh in chunks, discarding seeds; cut into cubes.
- In large bowl, combine melon cubes, berries, pineapple, peaches, pears, apples and grapes. Pour cooled syrup over fruit mixture. Refrigerate until ready to serve or for up to 4 hours.
- Just before serving, pile fruit mixture into melon basket. Spoon liqueur (if using) and accumulated juice over fruit and serve immediately. Makes about 16 servings.

Don't stop with just barbecued main dishes and vegetables. You can barbecue your dessert, too. On large buttered pieces of foil, place sliced peaches, nectarines, apples, pears or bananas; sprinkle with brown sugar, cinnamon, lemon juice or chopped nuts. Fold to make sealed packets and grill while you enjoy the first course. To serve, unwrap fruit onto individual dessert plates and pass cream, ice cream and liqueurs to complement the fruit, if desired.

Fruit-Filled Watermelon with Lemon-Lime Syrup

LAYERED RASPBERRY PARFAITS

Raspberry season is short, so capture their flavor in pretty parfaits.

1	envelope unflavored gelatin	1
1/4 cup	lemon juice	50 mL
3	eggs, separated	3
1/2 cup	granulated sugar	125 mL
1-1/4 cups	crushed raspberries	300 mL
1/2 cup	whipping cream, whipped	125 mL
3/4 cup	raspberries	175 mL
GARNISH:		
	Whipped cream	
	Raspberries	
	Mint sprigs	

• In small saucepan, sprinkle gelatin over lemon juice and let stand for a few minutes to soften; heat over low heat until gelatin is dissolved.

• In top of double boiler, beat egg yolks with sugar until light and fluffy. Add crushed raspberries and gelatin mixture, stirring well. Cook over hot water until thickened. Let cool thoroughly until mixture begins to set. Mix well.

• In bowl, beat egg whites until stiff peaks form; gently fold into raspberry mixture. Fold in whipped cream.

• Spoon about 1/3 cup (75 mL) of the raspberry mixture into each of 6 parfait glasses. Divide whole raspberries equally among glasses and cover with remaining raspberry mixture. Chill until set.

• **Garnish:** At serving time, garnish each serving with whipped cream, raspberries and mint. Makes 6 servings.

VARIATION:

LAYERED STRAWBERRY PARFAITS:
• Substitute 1-1/4 cups (300 mL) puréed strawberries for the crushed raspberries and 3/4 cup (175 mL) sliced strawberries for the raspberries in parfait. Garnish with whole berries.

STRAWBERRY CREAM PUFFS WITH CUSTARD CREAM FILLING

The custard can be made ahead, but the puffs should be baked and served the same day. For best results, don't use nonstick baking sheets.

CREAM PUFFS:		
3/4 cup	water	175 mL
1/3 cup	butter	75 mL
3/4 cup	all-purpose flour	175 mL
Pinch	salt	Pinch
3	eggs	3
CUSTARD CREAM FILLING:		
3 tbsp	granulated sugar	50 mL
1 tbsp	cornstarch	15 mL
1 cup	light cream	250 mL
2	egg yolks	2
1/2 tsp	vanilla	2 mL
1/2 cup	whipping cream	125 mL
1-1/2 cups	sliced hulled strawberries	375 mL
	Icing sugar	

• **Cream Puffs:** In heavy saucepan, combine water with butter over high heat; bring to boil. Reduce heat to low; add flour and salt, stirring vigorously with wooden spoon until mixture forms smooth ball that leaves side of pan. Remove from heat.

• Add eggs, one at a time, beating vigorously with electric mixer after each addition; continue beating until dough is smooth and shiny. Gather dough into ball in pan; refrigerate for 15 minutes.

• Divide dough into 6 portions, dropping each onto lightly greased baking sheet and mounding high in centre. Bake in 425°F (220°C) oven for 15 minutes; reduce heat to 350°F (180°C) and bake for 25 to 30 minutes longer or until well puffed, crisp and golden. Let cool completely on racks.

• **Custard Cream Filling:** In heavy saucepan, mix sugar with cornstarch. Whisk in light cream and egg yolks. Bring to boil over medium heat, stirring constantly; cook for 1 minute or until thickened. Remove from heat; stir in vanilla. Pour into bowl, place plastic wrap or waxed paper directly on surface of custard and refrigerate until cold.

• Just before serving, whip whipping cream; fold into chilled custard.

• Cut thin slice from top of each cream puff. Remove any moist bits of dough inside. Fill each puff with berries and custard filling.

• Replace tops; dust with icing sugar. Serve immediately. Makes 6 servings.

Cream puffs are delicious filled simply with lightly sweetened whipped cream and topped with sliced, hulled berries. The cream may be flavored with a dash of cinnamon and the berries splashed with strawberry liqueur or an orange-flavored liqueur, if desired.

Layered Strawberry Parfait

STRAWBERRY AND HAZELNUT TORTE

This spectacular dessert is a unique combination of strawberries, enormous hazelnut cookie rounds and whipped cream.

1 cup	hazelnuts	250 mL
1/2 cup	butter	125 mL
1/2 cup	granulated sugar	125 mL
3/4 cup	(approx) all-purpose flour	175 mL
1 cup	whipping cream	250 mL
2 tbsp	icing sugar	25 mL
2 tbsp	hazelnut-flavored liqueur	25 mL
2-1/2 cups	strawberries, hulled	625 mL
	Mint leaves	

• Spread hazelnuts on baking sheet; toast in 350°F (180°C) oven for 10 to 15 minutes or until skins loosen. Transfer to clean terry tea towel; rub to remove most of the skins. Let cool completely. In food processor and using on/off motion, chop hazelnuts very finely.

• In bowl, cream butter with sugar until light and fluffy. Using wooden spoon, gradually stir in flour and hazelnuts, blending well and adding 2 tbsp (25 mL) more flour if dough is shiny or greasy.

• Using back of spoon, press half of the dough into waxed paper-lined 9-inch (1.5 L) round cake pan. Invert onto ungreased baking sheet; remove waxed paper. Repeat with remaining dough. Using fingertips or fork, flute edges of cookies decoratively if desired.

• Bake cookies, one at a time, in 375°F (190°C) oven for 12 to 14 minutes or until lightly golden. While still warm, cut one of the cookies into 8 wedges. Let cool completely on baking sheets. (Cookies can be made ahead and stored in airtight container for up to 3 days.)

• Set uncut cookie on serving plate. In chilled bowl, whip cream, icing sugar and liqueur. Spoon into pastry bag fitted with 1/4-inch (5 mm) star tip; pipe 8 spokes onto uncut cookie.

• Reserve one perfect strawberry for garnish. Halve remaining berries and arrange, cut sides down, between spokes of whipped cream.

• Press cookie wedges into whipped cream so that wedges rest on berries at 45° angle, creating pinwheel effect (see photo).

• Pipe rosettes of whipped cream decoratively between wedges and at centre; place whole berry in centre. Garnish with mint leaves. Makes 8 servings.

ESPRESSO MOUSSE WITH MOCHA CREAM

Anyone who likes coffee will love this light dessert.

1 tsp	unflavored gelatin	5 mL
3/4 cup	cold strong espresso	175 mL
3	eggs, separated	3
1/4 cup	granulated sugar	50 mL
2 oz	semisweet chocolate, cut in small chunks	60 g
3/4 cup	whipping cream, whipped	175 mL
1/2 tsp	vanilla	2 mL
MOCHA CREAM:		
1/2 cup	whipping cream	125 mL
1 tbsp	icing sugar	15 mL
1 tsp	instant coffee powder	5 mL
GARNISH:		
	Unsweetened cocoa powder	
	Shaved chocolate (optional)	

Spoon Espresso Mousse into a chocolate crumb crust and refrigerate for at least 4 hours, or overnight, until firm. Top with Mocha Cream; garnish with a sprinkle of cocoa or shaved chocolate.

To make Chocolate Crumb Crust: Mix together 1 cup (250 mL) chocolate cookie crumbs, 2 tbsp (25 mL) granulated sugar and 1/4 cup (50 mL) melted butter. Press evenly onto bottom and sides of 9-inch (23 cm) pie plate. Bake in 350°F (180°C) oven for 8 minutes or alternatively, microwave, uncovered, at High for 2 minutes. Set aside to cool.

• In small bowl, sprinkle gelatin over 1/4 cup (50 mL) of the espresso; let stand for a few minutes to soften.

• In saucepan, beat egg yolks. Blend in remaining espresso, sugar and chocolate; cook over medium-low heat, stirring constantly, for about 5 minutes or until chocolate has melted and mixture thickened. Do not boil. Remove from heat; stir in gelatin mixture, stirring until gelatin has dissolved. Let cool to room temperature. Fold in whipped cream and vanilla.

• Beat egg whites until stiff peaks form; fold into espresso mixture. Spoon into 4 large wine glasses; cover and refrigerate for several hours or until firm, or overnight.

• **Mocha Cream:** Up to 1 hour before serving, beat together cream, sugar and instant coffee just until cream is slightly thickened. Spoon over mousse, completely covering each serving.

• **Garnish:** Through fine sieve, sprinkle mocha cream with cocoa; garnish with shaved chocolate (if using). Makes 4 servings.

KIWI TORTE

Bright green kiwifruit tops this light-tasting cake which is filled with hazelnuts and whipped cream. It's impressive, yet easy to make. (photo, p.138)

5	eggs, separated	5
3/4 cup	granulated sugar	175 mL
1/4 cup	unsweetened cocoa powder	50 mL
1/2 cup	ground hazelnuts	125 mL
1 tsp	baking powder	5 mL
	Icing sugar	
1-1/2 cups	whipping cream	375 mL
1/2 cup	icing sugar	125 mL
1 tsp	vanilla	5 mL
4	kiwifruit	4
1/4 cup	apple jelly	50 mL

• Line greased 15- x 10-inch (2 L) jelly roll pan with waxed paper; set aside.

• In large bowl, beat egg yolks, 1/2 cup (125 mL) of the granulated sugar and cocoa for about 5 minutes or until thickened. In separate bowl, beat egg whites until soft peaks form; gradually beat in remaining granulated sugar until stiff peaks form. Fold into egg yolk mixture along with hazelnuts and baking powder. Spread batter evenly in prepared pan.

• Bake in 350°F (180°C) oven for 15 to 20 minutes or until cake comes away from edges of pan. Place clean tea towel on wire rack and dust with icing sugar. Turn out cake onto towel and carefully remove waxed paper. Let cool for 20 minutes.

• Whip cream with 1/2 cup (125 mL) icing sugar; beat in vanilla. Spread over cake and cut lengthwise into 4 strips. Roll up one strip, starting from short end, and place cut side up on serving plate. Wrap remaining strips, cream side in, around centre roll.

• Peel kiwifruit; cut into 1/4-inch (5 mm) thick slices and halve. Arrange slices in overlapping concentric circles to cover top of cake. Fan out slices in centre.

• In small saucepan, melt apple jelly and brush over kiwifruit to prevent fruit from drying out. Refrigerate for at least 2 hours before serving. Cake is best when served the same day. Refrigerate any leftover cake. Makes 6 to 8 servings.

TROPICAL CHEESECAKE WITH GINGER-COCONUT CRUST

Use a variety of fruits—tropical or local—and let your creativity flow when you design your own colorful topping for this easy cheesecake.

CRUST:		
1-2/3 cups	gingersnap crumbs*	400 mL
1/2 cup	unsweetened desiccated coconut	125 mL
2 tsp	grated fresh gingerroot	10 mL
1/2 cup	unsalted butter, melted	125 mL
FILLING:		
1 lb	cream cheese	500 g
1 cup	sour cream	250 mL
3/4 cup	granulated sugar	175 mL
5	eggs	5
2 tbsp	all-purpose flour	25 mL
1 tsp	vanilla	5 mL
GLAZE AND TOPPING:		
1/3 cup	apricot jam	75 mL
1 tbsp	water	15 mL
2	kiwifruit	2
1	banana	1
Half	papaya	Half

• **Crust:** In small bowl, mix together crumbs, coconut and gingerroot. Drizzle with melted butter; stir and toss until combined and no dry crumbs remain. Press onto bottom of ungreased 10-inch (3 L) springform pan. Set aside.
• **Filling:** In food processor or with electric mixer, break up cream cheese slightly. Add sour cream, sugar, eggs, flour and vanilla; process just until blended and smooth. Pour over crust; bake in 325°F (160°C) oven for about 1-1/4 hours or until centre of cake is almost firm to the touch. Remove from oven and immediately run sharp knife around inside of pan. Let cool on wire rack.
• **Glaze and Topping:** In small saucepan, heat apricot jam with water until melted. Set aside.
• Peel and slice kiwifruit, banana and papaya into 1/4-inch (5 mm) thick slices. Arrange papaya slices around outside of cake, then ring of kiwifruit slices on inside; fan out banana slices in centre. Brush with warm apricot glaze. Cover and refrigerate for at least 4 hours or overnight. Remove sides of pan and transfer to serving plate. Makes about 10 servings.
* You'll need about 24 gingersnaps.

CHILLED MOULDED CHEESECAKES

Easy-to-make cheesecakes are a smooth lemony finish to a summer meal.

1	envelope unflavored gelatin	1
1/4 cup	water	50 mL
2	egg yolks	2
1/2 cup	icing sugar	125 mL
1/2 lb	cream cheese, softened	250 g
2 tbsp	lemon juice	25 mL
1 tsp	vanilla	5 mL
1 cup	light cream	250 mL
	Cherries	

• In saucepan, sprinkle gelatin over water. Let stand for 1 minute to soften. Bring just to boil, stirring until gelatin dissolves; set aside.
• In mixing bowl, beat together egg yolks, sugar, cream cheese, lemon juice and vanilla. Stir cream into gelatin mixture; gradually beat into cream cheese mixture until smooth. Divide among six rinsed but not dried 3/4-cup (175 mL) moulds. Cover and refrigerate for 2 hours or until set.
• To serve, unmould onto serving platter or individual plates and garnish with cherries. Makes 6 servings.

(Clockwise from top) Kiwi Torte (p. 137); Tropical Cheesecake with Ginger-Coconut Crust; Orange Chiffon Roll with Mango-Lime Curd (p. 140)

ORANGE CHIFFON ROLL WITH MANGO-LIME CURD

This dessert is for those who like something special but not too sweet. (photo, p.138)

MANGO-LIME CURD:

2	mangoes	2
1/3 cup	granulated sugar	75 mL
1/3 cup	butter	75 mL
2 tbsp	lime juice	25 mL
1 tsp	grated lime rind	5 mL
4	egg yolks, lightly beaten	4

ORANGE CHIFFON ROLL:

1 cup	all-purpose flour	250 mL
3/4 cup	granulated sugar	175 mL
1-1/2 tsp	baking powder	7 mL
1/2 tsp	salt	2 mL
1/3 cup	orange juice	75 mL
1/4 cup	vegetable oil	50 mL
2	egg yolks	2
1 tbsp	grated orange rind	15 mL
1/2 tsp	vanilla	2 mL
6	egg whites	6
1/4 tsp	cream of tartar	1 mL
	Icing sugar	

GARNISH:

	Orange peel
	Mango slices
	Orange leaves (optional)

• **Mango-Lime Curd:** Peel and pit mangoes; chop finely. In heavy saucepan over medium heat, cook mangoes, uncovered, for about 10 minutes or until softened, stirring often. Transfer to food processor or blender; process until smooth. Return to saucepan and stir in sugar, butter, lime juice and rind. Stir in egg yolks; cook over low heat, stirring constantly, for 8 to 10 minutes or until thickened. Let cool, stirring frequently. Place plastic wrap on surface of curd and refrigerate for at least 4 hours before using. (Curd can be prepared several days ahead and refrigerated.)

• **Orange Chiffon Roll:** Line greased 15- x 10-inch (2 L) jelly roll pan with waxed paper; set aside.

• In large bowl, stir together flour, 1/2 cup (125 mL) of the granulated sugar, baking powder and salt. Make well in middle; add orange juice, oil, egg yolks, orange rind and vanilla. Stir until smooth. (Mixture may be slightly stiff.)

• In large bowl, beat egg whites until soft peaks form; add cream of tartar and beat until stiff. Gradually beat in remaining 1/4 cup (50 mL) granulated sugar. Whisk one-quarter of the egg white mixture into egg yolk mixture, then fold in remaining egg white mixture. Spread batter evenly in prepared pan.

• Bake in 325°F (160°C) oven for 20 to 25 minutes or until cake springs back when lightly touched. Place clean tea towel on wire rack and sprinkle with icing sugar. Turn out cake onto towel and carefully remove waxed paper. Trim hard edges of cake and roll up cake in towel, starting at short end. Let cool for 30 minutes. Unroll, spread with Mango-Lime Curd and roll up again.

• **Garnish:** Place roll, seam side down, on serving platter. Garnish with orange peel, mango slices, and orange leaves (if using). Makes 6 to 8 servings.

HONEY-YOGURT SAUCE

Sweet yogurt sauce with a hint of orange makes a delicious summer dessert when served with raspberries and peaches.

1 cup	plain yogurt	250 mL
2 tbsp	liquid honey	25 mL
2 tsp	orange juice	10 mL
1/4 tsp	finely grated orange rind	1 mL

• In small bowl, stir together yogurt, honey, orange juice and rind. Makes about 1 cup (250 mL).

FROZEN YOGURT VARIATIONS

Frozen Strawberry Yogurt: Substitute 3 cups (750 mL) or about 1 lb (500 g) hulled strawberries for peaches. Substitute orange juice for lemon juice. Prepare as directed in Frozen Peach Yogurt recipe.

Frozen Banana-Blueberry Yogurt: Substitute 1-1/2 cups (375 mL) blueberries and 1 sliced banana for peaches. Prepare as directed in Frozen Peach Yogurt recipe.

Frozen Peach Yogurt

FROZEN PEACH YOGURT

Depending on your ice-cream machine, or the temperature of the frozen fruit if using the food processor method, the frozen yogurt may be too soft to serve immediately. Transfer to chilled storage container and freeze until firm. About 30 minutes before serving, transfer yogurt to refrigerator to soften slightly.

3 cups	sliced peaches (about 1 lb/500 g or 4 medium)	750 mL
1/3 cup	fruit/berry sugar	75 mL
1/2 cup	plain yogurt	125 mL
1 tbsp	lemon juice	15 mL

• **Ice-Cream Maker Method:** In food processor or blender, process peaches until puréed. Add sugar, yogurt and lemon juice; process until well blended. Transfer to ice-cream maker and freeze following manufacturer's instructions. Serve immediately or transfer to storage container and freeze for up to 1 week.

• **Food-Processor Method:** At least 5 hours before serving, place peaches in single layer on baking sheet; cover and freeze until solid. In food processor, combine frozen peaches with sugar. Using on/off motion, process until coarsely chopped. Stir together yogurt and lemon juice. With machine running, gradually pour in yogurt mixture through feed tube. Process until smooth and creamy, redistributing chunks of fruit if necessary.

• Serve immediately or transfer to storage container and freeze for up to 1 week. Makes about 3 cups (750 mL).

TUILES WITH STRAWBERRY ICE CREAM AND CHOCOLATE SAUCE

Combine two favorite flavors in a tasty cookie cup for a summery make-ahead dessert which you assemble just before serving.

TUILES:

2	egg whites	2
1/2 cup	granulated sugar	125 mL
1/3 cup	all-purpose flour	75 mL
1/4 cup	unsalted butter, melted	50 mL
2 tsp	water	10 mL
1 tsp	almond extract	5 mL
4 cups	strawberry ice cream (recipe opposite page)	1 L

CHOCOLATE SAUCE:

2/3 cup	granulated sugar	150 mL
1/2 cup	unsweetened cocoa powder	125 mL
1/2 cup	water	125 mL
1/2 cup	butter	125 mL
1 tsp	vanilla	5 mL

• **Tuiles:** In bowl, whisk together egg whites, sugar, flour, melted butter, water and almond extract just until blended. Using 2 to 3 tbsp (25 to 45 mL) batter for each tuile, drop batter onto greased and floured baking sheets, making only 3 on each sheet. Gently spread batter into 6-inch (15 cm) circles. Bake one sheet at a time in 400°F (200°C) oven for 6 to 8 minutes or until edges are just beginning to brown.

• Using spatula, immediately drape each tuile over inverted custard cup or glass, gently pressing to flute edges. Let cool. Repeat with remaining batter. Store in airtight container for up to 2 days.

• **Chocolate Sauce:** In saucepan, combine sugar and cocoa. Blend in water and cook over medium heat, stirring constantly, until mixture comes to boil. Reduce heat and boil gently for 5 minutes. Remove from heat; stir in butter and vanilla. Let cool and store in refrigerator for up to 2 days.

• To serve, spoon about 2 tbsp (25 mL) chocolate sauce into each tuile. Top with small scoop of ice cream. Makes 8 servings.

Tuile with Strawberry Ice Cream and Chocolate Sauce

EASY STRAWBERRY ICE CREAM

This fresh berry treat can be prepared without an ice-cream maker, although the texture will be smoother if you use one. Either way, the homemade flavor is unbeatable.

1 cup	light cream	250 mL
2/3 cup	granulated sugar	150 mL
1/4 cup	skim milk powder	50 mL
1 cup	whipping cream	250 mL
4 cups	strawberries, hulled	1 L

• In saucepan, combine light cream, sugar and skim milk powder. Cook over medium heat, stirring occasionally, until sugar dissolves. Remove from heat; let cool.

• In large bowl, combine sugar mixture with whipping cream. In food processor or blender, purée half of the berries. Slice remaining berries thinly. Stir sliced and puréed berries into cream mixture until well blended. Cover and freeze for 2 hours. (If using ice-cream maker, freeze according to manufacturer's instructions.)

• Using electric mixer, beat strawberry mixture until slushy. Cover and return to freezer for 1 hour or until frozen to desired consistency. If ice cream is too solid to scoop easily, soften in refrigerator for 15 to 30 minutes before serving. Makes about 4 cups (1 L).

For the Piña Colada Cheesecake crust, make cookie crumbs from any plain cookie, such as vanilla wafers, shortbread types or digestives; crush in food processor or with rolling pin.

PIÑA COLADA CHEESECAKE

There's nothing like a taste of piña colada to make you feel summery. This light dessert is no-bake easy. (photo, p.8)

1 cup	fine dry cookie crumbs	250 mL
1 cup	flaked coconut	250 mL
1/4 cup	butter, melted	50 mL
1	can (14 oz/398 mL) crushed pineapple	1
1/4 cup	light rum	50 mL
1	envelope unflavored gelatin	1
3	egg yolks	3
1 cup	granulated sugar	250 mL
1/4 tsp	salt	1 mL
1/2 cup	coconut milk*	125 mL
1 lb	cream cheese	500 g
3	egg whites	3

GARNISH (optional):

	Shredded fresh coconut, sliced fresh pineapple	

• Mix together cookie crumbs, coconut and melted butter. Reserve 1/2 cup (125 mL) for topping; press remainder into bottom of 9-inch (23 cm) springform pan.

• Drain pineapple, reserving 1/2 cup (125 mL) juice; set pineapple aside. In small saucepan, combine pineapple juice with rum; sprinkle gelatin into liquid; stir over low heat until dissolved. Remove from heat and set aside.

• In small heavy saucepan, whisk together egg yolks, 3/4 cup (175 mL) of the sugar, salt and coconut milk. Cook over low heat, stirring constantly, until slightly thickened; do not boil. Add gelatin mixture.

• Beat cream cheese until smooth; beat in gelatin mixture. Stir in reserved pineapple; chill until very slightly thickened, stirring once or twice.

• Beat egg whites until soft peaks form; gradually beat in remaining 1/4 cup (50 mL) sugar until stiff peaks form. Fold into cream cheese mixture. Pour into prepared pan. Sprinkle reserved crumbs on top. Chill until set, at least 4 hours.

• **Garnish:** Top with fresh coconut and pineapple (if using). Makes about 10 servings.
*Coconut milk is available in cans from specialty shops and some supermarkets; if unavailable, use regular milk.

HONEYDEW LIME SORBET

Serve this pretty dessert in tall glasses or scalloped melon shells.

1/2 cup	granulated sugar	125 mL
1/2 cup	water	125 mL
3 cups	honeydew melon purée*	750 mL
1/4 cup	lime juice	50 mL
2 tbsp	tequila	25 mL
2 tsp	finely grated lime rind	10 mL
Pinch	salt	Pinch
GARNISH:		
	Green seedless grapes or lime slices	

• In saucepan, combine sugar and water; bring just to boil, stirring to dissolve sugar. Let cool completely; refrigerate until cold.

• In blender or food processor, blend melon purée, lime juice, tequila, lime rind, salt and cold sugar syrup. Freeze in ice-cream machine according to manufacturer's instructions. (Alternatively, pour mixture into 8-inch/2 L square pan. Freeze until almost firm, about 3 hours. Transfer to bowl or food processor; beat until fluffy. Pour back into pan and freeze until firm.) Let stand at room temperature for a few minutes before serving to soften slightly.

• **Garnish:** Scoop sorbet into sherbet glasses. Garnish with grapes. Makes about 4 cups (1 L).

*To make 3 cups (750 mL) melon purée, peel and halve honeydew melons (about 3 lb/1.5 kg); remove seeds and chop. Purée in blender or food processor.

FROZEN STRAWBERRY MOUSSE WITH STRAWBERRY SAUCE

This pretty red-and-white dessert celebrates strawberry season. (photo, p.147)

3	egg yolks	3
1/2 cup	granulated sugar	125 mL
1-1/2 cups	hot milk	375 mL
Pinch	salt	Pinch
1/4 cup	orange-flavored liqueur	50 mL
2 cups	whipping cream	500 mL
2 cups	coarsely chopped hulled strawberries	500 mL
STRAWBERRY SAUCE:		
2 cups	thinly sliced hulled strawberries	500 mL
1/4 cup	orange-flavored liqueur	50 mL
1 tbsp	lemon juice	15 mL

• In bowl, beat together egg yolks and sugar until thick and lemon colored; stir in milk and salt.

• Pour mixture into small heavy saucepan; cook over medium heat, stirring constantly, until mixture thickens slightly and coats back of spoon, about 5 minutes. Do not let mixture boil. Remove from heat and stir in liqueur. Place saucepan in ice cubes; chill for a few minutes or until cool.

• Whip cream and fold into chilled egg mixture. Pour into shallow metal pan and freeze just until almost firm, stirring occasionally. Remove from freezer and beat with electric mixer or in food processor until slushy. (Alternatively, freeze in ice-cream machine according to manufacturer's instructions.) Fold in chopped strawberries.

• Pour mixture into 6-cup (1.5 L) serving bowl and freeze until top becomes firm. Cover with plastic wrap and freeze for 4 to 5 hours or until firm. Before serving, let soften slightly in refrigerator or at room temperature.

• **Strawberry Sauce:** Combine sliced strawberries, liqueur and lemon juice; let stand at room temperature for 1 hour before serving. Serve with mousse. Makes 6 to 8 servings.

If you do not wish to use alcohol in recipes, you can substitute a similar flavor without using liqueurs.

• For orange liqueurs, such as Grand Marnier, Triple Sec or Cointreau, use an equivalent amount of frozen orange juice concentrate. Adding a little finely grated orange rind intensifies the orange flavor.

• For coffee liqueurs, such as Tia Maria or Kahlua, use an equivalent amount of extra-strong coffee.

• For kirsch or other cherry liqueurs, try strawberry or raspberry frozen juice concentrate.

• For rum, substitute a small amount of artificial rum extract.

Honeydew Lime Sorbet

ICE CREAM SANDWICHES

Ice cream sandwiches used to be a popular treat at summer picnics and country fairs. Here's an updated version made by sandwiching squares of ice cream between big homemade oatmeal cookies. If you prefer unfrozen cookies, assemble the sandwiches just before serving.

2 cups	rolled oats	500 mL
1/2 tsp	baking soda	2 mL
1 cup	all-purpose flour	250 mL
1/4 tsp	cinnamon	1 mL
1/4 tsp	nutmeg	1 mL
1/4 tsp	salt	1 mL
1/2 cup	butter	125 mL
3/4 cup	packed brown sugar	175 mL
3/4 cup	granulated sugar	175 mL
2	eggs	2
1 tsp	vanilla	5 mL
1/2 cup	semisweet chocolate chips	125 mL
4 cups	vanilla ice cream (preferably in rectangular carton)	1 L

• In bowl, combine rolled oats, baking soda, flour, cinnamon, nutmeg and salt; mix well.
• In separate bowl, cream together butter and brown and granulated sugars until light and fluffy. Beat in eggs and vanilla. Gradually blend in dry ingredients. Stir in chocolate chips.
• Shape about 3 tbsp (50 mL) dough at a time into balls. Arrange well apart on baking sheets; press with fingertips into 3-inch (8 cm) circles to make 18 to 20 cookies, about 6 cookies per sheet. Bake in 350°F (180°C) oven for 12 to 14 minutes or until golden. Let cool on wire racks.
• To assemble sandwiches, cut ice cream into squares about 1/2-inch (1 cm) thick; sandwich between cookies. Arrange on baking sheet and freeze until solid; wrap individually in plastic wrap or foil. Makes 9 or 10 sandwiches.

STORING ICE-CREAM DESSERTS

If not serving the dessert as soon as it's frozen solid, wrap it well in plastic wrap or a couple of layers of foil; label and store it where it won't be crushed. For maximum flavor and texture, serve as soon as possible after freezing, preferably within one or two weeks. You may want to let the dessert soften slightly in the refrigerator or at room temperature before serving.

BANANA-YOGURT BOATS

Here's a dessert that's sure to be a hit with kids: tangy banana yogurt served in frozen banana skins, all drizzled with chocolate sauce and sprinkled with peanuts.

6	bananas (unpeeled)	6
2 tbsp	lemon juice	25 mL
1/4 cup	fruit/berry sugar	50 mL
2 cups	plain yogurt	500 mL
CHOCOLATE SAUCE:		
4 oz	semisweet chocolate	125 g
1 cup	light cream	250 mL
1/4 cup	corn syrup	50 mL
2 tbsp	butter	25 mL
GARNISH:		
1/2 cup	chopped peanuts	125 mL

• Slice off top third of bananas lengthwise. Carefully remove banana pulp from both parts, reserving bottom part of banana skins to form "boat." Place banana boats on baking sheet and freeze.
• In blender or food processor, combine banana pulp, lemon juice and sugar; process until puréed. Combine purée with yogurt; pour into shallow metal pan and freeze until firm, stirring occasionally. (Alternatively, freeze in ice-cream machine according to manufacturer's instructions.)
• Pipe or spoon mixture into frozen banana skins, mounding slightly. (There may be some mixture left; just freeze and save for another time.) Return filled boats to freezer and freeze until firm.
• **Chocolate Sauce:** In top of double boiler over hot not boiling water or in heavy saucepan over low heat, combine semisweet chocolate, cream, corn syrup and butter. Heat, stirring often, until chocolate has melted and sauce is smooth. Let cool and refrigerate.
• **Garnish:** At serving time, spoon Chocolate Sauce over bananas and sprinkle with peanuts. Makes 6 servings.

Chocolate Sauce can easily be made in the microwave oven. In an 8-cup (2 L) bowl, combine coarsely chopped semisweet chocolate, cream, corn syrup and butter. Microwave, uncovered, at High for about 3-1/2 minutes or until chocolate is melted and sauce is smooth, stirring twice. Let cool and refrigerate. Makes about 1-1/2 cups (375 mL).

(Clockwise from top) Ice Cream Sandwiches; Frozen Strawberry Mousse with Strawberry Sauce (p. 145); Frosted Orange; Banana-Yogurt Boat

FROSTED ORANGES

One of the most attractive ways to serve orange ice is in hollowed-out oranges. For a variation, use lemons, limes or even small grapefruits.

1 cup	water	250 mL
3/4 cup	granulated sugar	175 mL
6	seedless oranges	6
2 tbsp	lemon juice	25 mL
1 tbsp	grated orange rind	15 mL

• In saucepan, combine water with sugar. Bring to boil and boil for 4 minutes; let syrup cool.

• Cut 1/2-inch (1 cm) thick slice from one side of each orange; reserve slices. Remove pulp from each orange, being careful to leave rind intact; set rind shells aside.

• In blender or food processor, process pulp until puréed. Combine with cooled syrup, lemon juice and rind. Pour into shallow metal pan and freeze until very firm.

• Break up orange mixture with spoon and process in blender or food processor until slushy. (Alternatively, freeze in ice-cream machine according to manufacturer's instructions.)

• Spoon orange mixture into hollowed-out orange shells, mounding above rim; top with reserved orange slices, setting slightly askew. Place oranges in muffin tins to prevent tipping; freeze for 4 to 6 hours or until frozen solid.

• Immediately wrap oranges individually in plastic wrap or foil. Before serving, let soften slightly in refrigerator or at room temperature. Makes 6 servings.

Barbecue Basics

Barbecuing has come a long way in style and popularity. No longer content with occasional entrées charred over hot coals, smart outdoor cooks have learned to barbecue almost everything to perfection. Today's lifestyle includes entire meals cooked on the grill, from whole chickens to fish and seafood, from appetizers to fruits and vegetables. Many backyard chefs barbecue all year round. And we still love the taste and aroma of hamburgers and hotdogs for the family or the occasional sizzling steak. In this section, you'll find general information on the basics of barbecuing—from choosing the type of barbecue that's right for you to barbecuing hints and safety tips.

TYPES OF BARBECUES

Today barbecues are available in a variety of styles and designs, catering to every taste and budget. We've supplied you with a simple shopping guide and brief descriptions to help you select your barbecue.

CHARCOAL-FIRED BARBECUES

Open grills are generally speaking the most basic and least expensive barbecues. They come in a variety of sizes, from tabletop portables to more

Tabletop Grill

elaborate models featuring spit-roasting equipment, half hoods or windscreens. Smaller models, such as the **hibachi**, are the most portable for picnics and camping. Ideal for cooking steaks,

hamburgers, small fish, chops and chicken pieces, these units work well with foods that lie flat. Many feature a cooking grill that can be raised or lowered to adjust the heat.

Built-in brick barbecues belong to this

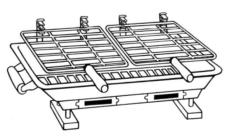

Hibachi

category of barbecues because like grills they're designed for open-cooking over direct heat.

Covered barbecues (kettle or box-shaped) are also available in many sizes and are very versatile. Cooking can be done with the lid open or closed, either directly on the grill or on a spit attachment. Ideal for windy or cold days, the closed units cook faster and seem to add a more intense smoke flavor. When closed, they function like an oven, eliminating the need for a rotisserie,

although this is often an option. Uncovered, they act as an open grill. Covered, food cooks quickly and requires less watching and turning, flare-ups are minimal and less charcoal is used.

Box-shaped barbecues with hinged lids generally function the same way covered kettles do.

Covered Kettle Barbecue

GAS AND ELECTRIC BARBECUES

Gas and electric barbecues also come in a variety of sizes and work on the same principle as covered kettles. Outdoor units using propane gas usually roll on wheels, while natural gas units, whether wagon-type or mounted on a fixed pedestal, need to be connected to a permanent gas line. Electric units are portable; they can simply be plugged into the nearest three-prong AC outlet.

These barbecues present many advantages. You don't have the work of

Electric Grill

building a fire and cleaning up the ashes. Most units require only a brief preheating. It's easy to maintain a constant temperature as long as there is a supply of power, be it gas or electricity. Deluxe gas models feature a temperature thermometer on the outside of the lid and large removable

shelves that provide convenient serving and work areas. Many of the larger models have two or more burners, offering the versatility of direct or indirect cooking. Recent additions include an automatic sparking unit which eliminates the need for matches, multi-level grills and side-burners that allow you to cook accompanying dishes or even make coffee.

While there is more temperature control with gas or electric barbecues, foods grilled on gas or electric barbecues cook in about the same time as on charcoal-fired models.

Built-in indoor grills are a terrific feature to have in your kitchen for year-round use. The recipes in this book that are cooked quickly over direct heat can also be prepared on an indoor grill.

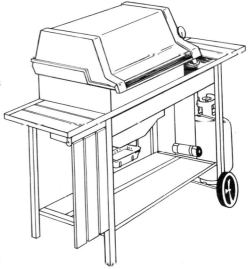

Gas Barbecue

TOOLS AND ACCESSORIES

INDISPENSABLE HELPERS

• Long-handled tongs with smooth tips to turn food gently without tearing.
• A long-handled fork.
• Extra-long, fire-proof (preferably asbestos) oven mitts.
• A long-handled basting brush.
• A long-handled broad metal spatula.
• A hinged wire basket for holding and turning small items, e.g. shrimp, fish fillets.
• A meat thermometer.
• A spray bottle for dousing flare-ups.
• A long butane lighter (shaped like a gun) is a safe fire-starting device. You may opt instead for an electric starter if you have an outlet nearby.

• A drip pan; this can be a disposable aluminum pan or a shallow metal baking pan wrapped in heavy foil.
• A stiff metal (or wire) brush for cleaning the rack or grill.
• A non-metallic marinade dish.
• A set of good sharp knives.
• Heavy foil.

OPTIONAL HELPERS

• A hinged, rectangular grilling basket for foods that require regular turning or may stick to rack.
• A rotisserie—electric or battery-operated—for ribs, chickens, roasts.
• Flat broiling rotisserie baskets to fit on the spit.
• A second pair of heavy, long-handled tongs for moving coals.

• Griddles for sausages and pancakes.
• Corn and potato holders.
• Skewers: stainless steel, flat-bladed skewers are best for meat. Wooden skewers (soak first in water for 30 minutes to prevent burning) are ideal for kabobs and vegetables.
• A rib rack.
• A V-shaped rack for holding chickens, hams, roasts.
• A utensil rack that clips onto the edge of the barbecue to hold tools.
• An all-weather cover for the barbecue to be stored outdoors.
• A grill-surface thermometer.

FUELS

Always consult your owner's manual before you begin to cook on any barbecue.

GAS (NATURAL OR PROPANE)
Gas barbecues may use either natural or propane gas. Most of these barbecues employ as fuel ceramic briquettes, volcanic lava rocks or metal bars above the burner. Juices drip onto these, causing smoke to rise and flavor the food. Soaked wood chips in a foil pan may be placed over the heat to add a smoky flavor.

ELECTRICITY
Electric barbecues are portable and may be plugged into the nearest three-prong AC outlet.

CHARCOAL
Charcoal briquettes are the most commonly used fuel. Choose a good quality that light easily and heat in about 30 minutes.

Instant lighting charcoal briquettes are impregnated with a chemical starter and should light quickly; however, they still require 30 minutes to heat fully.

Lump charcoal, while faster to light, is uneven in size and may produce sparks and burn unevenly.

AROMATIC HARDWOODS (CHUNKS OR CHIPS)
Aromatic wood chips should be soaked in water for 30 minutes, then used in moderation, in combination with hot coals. Fist-sized chunks last longest for smoke cooking in a water smoker. Wood chips work well for smoke flavoring. Tossed on the hot coals or placed in a little water in a foil pan set on the lava rocks or flavor bars, each will add its own distinctive taste.

Mesquite is probably the best-known and most popular of these aromatic hardwoods. Mesquite gives a rich, woodsy taste to pork, beef and ribs.

Hickory is another favorite, imparting a tangy, Southern-style flavor to the food.

Oak, maple and **pecan** add a distinctive taste.

Fruitwoods like apple, cherry or orange impart a sweet, mild flavor.

Alder is delicate and fragrant. This is the ideal wood in chunks or chips for barbecuing salmon steaks and other fish, adding a subtle, memorable flavor.

COOKING TIMES AND TEMPERATURES

Cooking times vary widely. Wind, temperature, the size of the food and whether the barbecue is open or closed will all affect the cooking time. Barbecuing is a relaxed form of cooking and is not nearly as exact as some other cooking methods. Be prepared to wait.

Temperature is easily controlled in gas and electric barbecues. When cooking on any type of open grill, adjust the rack height, if possible. Raise it for longer, slower cooking; lower it to sear quickly. Coals are hottest when banked together; spread coals apart to lower heat. In a covered barbecue, regulate the air flow. Open the vents fully to cook food faster. To lower the temperature, close the vents halfway. To extinguish coals, close the vents completely. If cooking for over an hour, you may have to add additional charcoal. DO NOT ADD BRIQUETTES DOUSED WITH STARTER FLUID. THIS IS VERY DANGEROUS.

Barbecue recipes in this book give heat descriptions for charcoal barbecuing and settings for gas/electric barbecuing as well as tests for doneness. (For example, "Cook fish fillets over medium-hot coals or on medium-high setting until fish flakes easily with fork.") Grill surface thermometers are available and some covered barbecues have a fitted or built-in temperature gauge.

If your barbecue does not have a temperature gauge, you can use this hand test to determine approximate temperature. Carefully hold your hand, palm side down, 2 or 3 inches (5 or 8 cm) above the rack until the heat feels uncomfortable. Count the seconds you can keep your hand in place. The following rule works quite well:

Number of seconds hand held over fire	Temperature
5 seconds	Low
4 seconds	Medium
3 seconds	Medium-High
2 seconds	High

STARTING THE FIRE

If you are using a charcoal barbecue, pile charcoal pyramid-style in the centre of the barbecue. Use a recommended electric starter or fuel (not gasoline or other flammable material) and ignite. Remove the electric starter as specified in manufacturer's instructions. When white ash has formed on the coals (usually after 40 to 45 minutes), spread out coals.

Build a fire that is the right size for what you're cooking. Use 12 to 24 briquettes for a few chops, hamburgers or hotdogs; 30 to 40 for a roast, adding more coals when needed.

To reduce flare-ups and to lower the temperature of a charcoal barbecue, raise the grill rack (if possible), spread coals apart or remove coals. To increase the temperature, tap ashes off with tongs, move coals closer together, add briquettes or lower grill rack.

For lighting and preheating gas and electric barbecues, follow manufacturer's instructions.

FLAVORING FOOD WITH SMOKE

Flavoring foods with the smoke of fragrant woods is an ancient cooking art that has recently gained popularity. In this book, we describe and provide recipes for two techniques for imparting smoke flavor to food. Quick smoke flavoring can be accomplished in any covered barbecue (p. 84); smoke cooking requires a smoker (p. 52).

Water Smoker

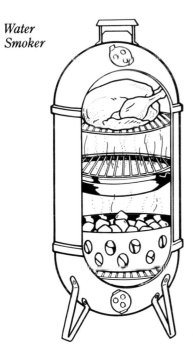

SMOKE COOKING
A **water smoker** looks like a covered cylinder-shaped barbecue. The water smoker uses a combination of low moist heat along with smoke to cook foods slowly and evenly. The fire pan holds a few hot coals as well as soaked wood chunks; the hardwood types, such as mesquite or hickory are best. A water pan, filled with hot liquid and sometimes seasonings, is placed above the coals. Food is placed on the grill rack above and the smoker is covered.

We've included tips for curing your food to enhance the smoked flavor as well as directions for smoke cooking on page 52.

SMOKE FLAVORING
You can achieve the rich color, woodsy taste and juiciness of smoke cooking even if you don't have a smoker. You can add a smoke flavor in any covered barbecue by adding dampened wood chips to the coals or by using a few drops of liquid smoke in a marinade.

Use chips or chunks of hardwoods or fruitwoods such as mesquite, hickory, oak, alder, walnut, maple, cherry, peach, or grapevine clippings (that have not been sprayed with chemicals). Don't use softwoods like pine or spruce which give off an unpleasant flavor. Soak wood chips in water for 30 minutes and chunks for one to two hours. Scatter a few damp chips directly onto the hot coals or lava rocks just before barbecuing. If you are long-cooking a large roast or turkey in a gas barbecue, place soaked chips or chunks in a foil pan set inside another foil pan containing some water; place the pan underneath the cooking rack.

Other flavoring agents impart good flavors to barbecued foods, too. Crack nuts with a hammer before soaking and adding to coals or lava rocks. Dried seaweed can be used for fish. Herbs and spices (whole cinnamon sticks, whole nutmeg, garlic cloves, dried orange peel or lemon peel) can be soaked and then sprinkled over coals or lava rocks for added flavor.

DIRECT VS INDIRECT HEAT

Direct heat means the food is cooked directly over the heat source or hot coals. The barbecue may be open or covered. Direct heat produces a quick cooking with more browning on the outside. Most barbecue enthusiasts prefer this method for steaks, chops and burgers.

Direct Heat

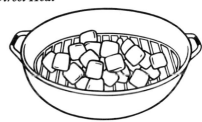

The indirect method is used to cook roasts, poultry and thick foods in covered barbecues without the food being directly over the heat source or hot coals. In the case of gas barbecues with two burners, one burner is lit, then the food is placed on the opposite side,

Indirect Heat

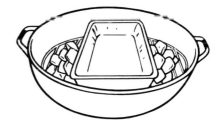

away from the heat source. The heat from the burner then warms the barbecue like an oven, avoiding any flare-ups. If using a covered charcoal barbecue, you can cook indirectly by placing hot coals around a drip pan, which must be slightly larger than the food being cooked. The food is then placed over the drip pan and the lid is closed; once again, flare-ups are prevented.

CHOOSING THE RIGHT FOODS FOR THE BARBECUE

The barbecue is incredibly versatile. Most cooks know that steaks, chops, chicken pieces, hamburgers and hotdogs cook beautifully on the barbecue. Any camper can tell you there is nothing more tantalizing than fresh fish over an open fire. Any fish that will hold its shape is perfect for barbecuing. Less tender cuts of meat, after marinating, will barbecue deliciously on skewers, on a spit or just straight on the grill. Short ribs and spareribs, especially with our selected basting sauces, are a taste treat. Vegetables, too, when properly barbecued are full of flavor—fresh young corn in its husks, potatoes in their skins. Or try your hand at some of our barbecued fruits.

MARINATING

Foods are marinated before barbecuing for two reasons. Firstly, the flavor is enhanced by herbs, garlic, spices or other aromatic ingredients in the marinade. Secondly, a tenderizer such as wine, vinegar, soy sauce or lemon juice will transform even the less tender cuts of meat into juicy, delicious dishes. See the Marinades and Sauces section (pp. 92–99) as well as individual barbecue recipes in this book for terrific marinade recipes.

HELPFUL HINTS FOR MARINATING:

• Pierce the meat in several places.

• Cubes or strips of meat require 3 to 6 hours in the marinade.

• Steaks should be marinated overnight.

• Roasts need 24 hours for best results.

• Less tender cuts of meat—flank steak, short ribs—need 12 to 24 hours.

• Meat must be refrigerated while marinating.

• Turn the meat several times while it is marinating.

• Use a non-metallic dish or bowl with a close-fitting lid for marinating or use a plastic bag.

• For additional flavor, baste the meat with the marinade while it cooks.

• Match up your favorite marinade with your choice of meat, poultry or seafood or follow the suggested recipes in this book. An apple juice marinade is heavenly with pork. Wine and garlic tenderize beef. Lemon juice is ideal for fish. Lamb is juicy when marinated with garlic, rosemary and fresh mint.

TIPS FOR THE SMART BARBECUE COOK

• Assemble all equipment and sauces before you start to barbecue.

• Always brush the cold grill with oil to prevent food from sticking.

• Check food often when cooking as temperatures vary widely.

• Make sure food is evenly balanced on the rotisserie. Food should be secured to turn evenly as the rod turns.

• Trim excess fat from meat to prevent flare-ups. A thin strip of fat around the edge of the meat should be slashed several times to prevent curling.

• To tenderize and add flavor, marinate food before barbecuing. Always remove food from refrigerator 30 minutes before cooking.

• To prevent scorching, use tomato or sugar-based sauces only during the last 15 minutes of cooking.

• For direct heat method, distribute the hot coals evenly over the bottom grid.

• For indirect heat method, arrange hot coals on either side of a drip pan placed in the centre of bottom grid. The pan can be made out of a double thickness of heavy-duty foil.

• Toss a few damp hickory chips onto the charcoal to give food an extra smoky flavor. To dampen chips, soak in water for 30 minutes.

• Soak wooden skewers for 30 minutes to prevent burning.

• Use stainless steel, flat-bladed skewers to facilitate turning large kabobs partway through cooking. Round skewers often create a hole in foods so that the skewer turns, but food chunks do not.

• Always use heavy, fire-proof oven mitts and long-handled tools.

• Always keep a spray bottle of water beside the barbecue to extinguish flare-ups.

• Turn food with long tongs. A fork will pierce food, releasing juices.

• Salt food after cooking to prevent dry food.

• To test thick steaks, roasts or poultry for doneness, insert a meat thermometer in the thickest part, not touching bone. Repeat in several places.

• Check for doneness (steaks, chops etc.) by making a small cut into the centre of the food.

• Never leave the thermometer in food on a barbecue.

• To make a foil drip pan: Using 18-inch (45 cm) wide heavy foil, tear off two sheets. Turn up the edges 1-1/2 inches (4 cm) on all sides, then pinch the corners together to form triangular shapes. Fold the corners to the sides of the pan, making them even with the sides. Fold over top of foil edge.

BARBECUING SAFETY

Enjoy your barbecue to the fullest but remember these important safety tips:

• Never use a charcoal barbecue indoors; the results can be fatal.

• Keep the barbecue away from dry grass or other fire hazards.

• Never use gasoline, kerosene, or alcohol to light charcoal. An explosion could occur.

• Never use starter fluid on hot (or even warm) coals. The fire will blaze up, and may cause serious injury.

• Trim as much visible fat from foods as possible. Dripping fat can cause flare-ups.

• Never allow children near the barbecue without adult supervision and never leave the barbecue during heating or cooking time if it is in a location accessible to children.

• Never leave the coals burning when you are finished barbecuing.

• Always handle foods and coals wearing fire-proof oven mitts and using long-handled utensils.

• Always keep a spray bottle filled with water beside the barbecue to douse flare-ups. Spray gently. If the barbecue has a cover, close it if a flare-up occurs.

• When using a gas or electric barbecue, always follow manufacturer's instructions.

• Never light a gas barbecue with the lid shut.

• Never store propane cylinders in an enclosed area, in sunlight, or within reach of children. Always store them upright.

Acknowledgments and Credits

The remaining recipes in this cookbook, as well as the handy charts and hints, were developed in the *Canadian Living* test kitchen by test kitchen manager **Patricia Jamieson** and her staff. Special thanks to staff members **Janet Cornish** and **Ruth Phelan**.

PHOTOGRAPHY CREDITS

Fred Bird: front and back covers; pages 8, 11, 12, 15, 19, 21, 23, 24, 26, 29, 31, 32, 38, 41, 42, 44, 46, 53, 54, 57, 58, 61, 63, 64, 66, 69, 70, 73, 75, 76, 79, 81, 82, 85, 86, 89, 90, 93, 94, 97, 98, 100, 102, 107, 111, 112, 114, 116, 119, 120, 123, 125, 128, 129, 131, 133, 135, 136, 138, 141, 142, 144, 147.
Chris Campbell: page 6.
Clive Champion: pages 104, 108.
Frank Grant: pages 2, 3, 7.
Clive Webster: pages 17, 34, 43, 132.
Robert Wigington: pages 49, 127.
Stanley Wong: page 37.

Food Styling Coordinator: **Margaret Fraser**

Food Stylists: **Jennifer McLagan**
Olga Truchan

Props Coordinator: **Debby Boyden**

The publisher would also like to thank Pottree & Pantree for use of the following props for photography:
Page 11: plastic cutlery; page 21: cutlery, plates and bowls; page 38: soup bowls.

Illustrator: **Elaine Macpherson**

Index

Design and Art Direction:	Gordon Sibley Design Inc.
Editorial:	Hugh Brewster Catherine Fraccaro
Editorial Assistance:	Shirley Knight Morris Beverley Renahan
Production:	Susan Barrable
Production Assistance:	Catherine A. Clark
Typography:	Attic Typesetting Inc.
Color Separation (front cover):	Colour Technologies
Color Separation:	La Cromolito
Printing and Binding:	New Interlitho S.p.A.
Advisory Board:	Robert A. Murray Carol Ferguson Margaret Fraser

THE RANDOM HOUSE
BARBECUE AND SUMMER FOODS COOKBOOK
was produced by Madison Press Books
under the direction of Albert E. Cummings.